James Joseph Sylvester

Principles of Versification

Exemplified in Metrical Translations

James Joseph Sylvester

Principles of Versification
Exemplified in Metrical Translations

ISBN/EAN: 9783741183522

Manufactured in Europe, USA, Canada, Australia, Japa

Cover: Foto ©Andreas Hilbeck / pixelio.de

Manufactured and distributed by brebook publishing software (www.brebook.com)

James Joseph Sylvester

Principles of Versification

THE

LAWS OF VERSE

OR

PRINCIPLES OF VERSIFICATION

Exemplified in Metrical Translations:

TOGETHER WITH AN ANNOTATED REPRINT OF

THE INAUGURAL PRESIDENTIAL ADDRESS TO THE
MATHEMATICAL AND PHYSICAL SECTION OF THE
BRITISH ASSOCIATION AT EXETER

BY

J. J. SYLVESTER, LL.D., F.R.S.

*Of the Institute of France, the Royal Academies of Science of Berlin, Göttingen,
Naples, Milan, &c. &c. &c.;
Examiner in Mathematics to the University of London.*

LONDON:
LONGMANS, GREEN, AND CO.
1870.

TO

MATTHEW ARNOLD, ESQ., D.C.L.

SOMEWHILE PROFESSOR OF POETRY AT THE UNIVERSITY OF OXFORD,

A CONSUMMATE MASTER OF THE ART,

IN GRATEFUL RECOGNITION OF

MUCH VALUABLE CRITICISM AND GENEROUS ENCOURAGEMENT

RECEIVED AT HIS HANDS,

I Dedicate

THIS ATTEMPT TO DISPLAY AND EXEMPLIFY

THE LAWS OF VERSE.

' Non ante volgatas per artes
  Verba loquor socianda chordis.'
                              HOR. *Car.* iv. 9.

By methods ne'er promulged before,
Fit speech o'er lyric chords I pour.

Παλαιὰ παροιμία ὅτι χαλεπὰ τὰ καλά ἐστιν ὅπῃ ἔχει μαθεῖν.
                              PLATO, *Socrat. in Cratylus.*

' Untwisting all the chains that tie
  The hidden soul of harmony.'
                              MILTON, *L'Allegro.*

PREFACE.

The technical or material part of versification (the art of rhythmical composition), like that of any other of the fine arts, is capable of being reduced to rules and referred to fixed principles.

I wish the title of LAWS OF VERSE, OR PRINCIPLES OF VERSIFICATION EXEMPLIFIED, to be understood in the sense of an attempt to illustrate this proposition by examples. This is not a treatise on Prosody, neither is it a discourse *de arte Poeticâ*. Moreover I do not profess to lay down a systematic body of doctrine on the Art of Versification, but merely to indicate, in the way of cursory comment, chiefly contained in notes to the text, the existence of such a doctrine, and the possibility of moulding it into a certain definite organic form. In poetry we have sound, thought, and words (i.e. thought clothed in sound); accordingly the subject falls naturally into three great divisions, the cogitative, the expressional, and the technical; to which we may give the respective names of Pneumatic, Linguistic, and Rhythmic. It is only with

Rhythm that I profess to deal. This again branches off into three principal branches—Metric, Chromatic, and Synectic.

Metric is concerned with Accent, Quantity, and Suspensions; the latter including the theories of Pauses, Rests, and Synthesis or Syllabic Groupings. I touch very briefly on this branch, accepting, in regard to it, the doctrine of Edgar Poe, given in his essay on the 'Rationale of Versification,' rendered, as I think, more complete by my introduction into it of the theory of the silent syllable or rest.

Metric is concerned with the discontinuous, Synectic with the continuous, aspect of the Art. Between the two lies Chromatic, which comprises the study of the qualities, affinities, and colorific properties of sound.* Into this part of the subject, except so far as occasionally glancing

---

* I notice that in Mr. Tom Hood's 'Rules of Rhyme' certain of the principles of Chromatic have been incidentally discussed and gone into (as regards the powers of initial consonants) in some detail. Chromatic may be studied with respect to Matter, Mode, and Relation. Its matter may be consonantal, vocal, or diphthongal; its mode may be taken with reference to congruity, opposition, and transition or modulation. As to relation, it may be regarded as a co-ordinate factor of Synectic or of Expression, or *per se*, i.e. with regard to the purely sensuous impression; which last, again, will bring under view the position as initial, terminal, or medial. This is a mere hasty and superficial view of the subject: in things of the fancy a little play of fancy may be permitted.

Preface. 11

at its existence and referring to its effects, I do not profess to enter.* My chief business is with Synectic.

This, also, on a slight examination, will be found to run into three channels—*Anastomosis, Symptosis,* and between them the main flood of Phonetic Syzygy.† But it may be asked preliminarily how can Symptosis, which deals with rhymes, assonances (including alliterations, so called), and clashes (this last comprising as well agreeable reiterations, or congruences, as unpleasant ones, i.e. jangles or jars), how, I say, can a theory dealing with discreet matter of this kind, come under the head of Synectic: but the answer is easy, for if the elements with which it deals, its *matter*, is discontinuous, not so is the object to

---

* I cannot resist the temptation of quoting here from a daily morning paper the following unconsciously chromatic passage descriptive of the total eclipse of the moon, that grand spectacle of nature, which I witnessed and watched yesternight from Woolwich Common in front of my house, which in a few days I am to quit:—' The last portion of the shadow of the earth had been passed through by the moon, which then again sailed "in its full orb of glory through the dark blue depth.' " The beauty of sound in this description is almost as delicious as the impression of the sight of nature which it recalls.

† I have heard of practical use being made by some to whom the report of it has reached of this salient principle of phonetic syzygy, alike for proving, correcting, and strengthening their verses. A lady also has conveyed to me through a mutual friend the conviction of the value and fertility of this principle, in its application to musical composition, which has forced itself on her

which it tends (its *form*); just, for instance, as in an iron shield or curtain or a trial target, the bolts and screws and rivets are separate, but serve to consolidate and bring into conjunction the plates, and to give cohesion and unity to the structure.

Anastomosis regards the junction of words, the laying of them duly alongside one another (like drainage pipes set end to end, or the capillary terminations of the veins and arteries) so as to

notice. I conceive that the method of triadic analysis which I have employed in the genesis and distribution of the principles of lyrical poetry, is founded on the nature of things and not on an arbitrary subjective rule of classification. I can honestly aver that I was not on the look-out for any such an arithmetical law, but that starting originally with phonetic syzygy alone as my distinctive principle, the connexions and ramifications which grew out of and around it, grouped themselves as it were spontaneously, according to this law of trichotomy, each joint of the arborescence at which I successively arrived in my analysis, throwing off from itself three branches. It may be the case that a similar ternary law of development would apply to music, painting, sculpture, in a word, to the elucidation of the higher principles of all the fine arts. Following out this clue it is conceivable that we might succeed in laying the foundations of a science of Comparative Aesthetic, or at least of a general Aesthetico-technic. Of one thing I have no doubt, which is, that when the analysis of principles which I have here faintly indicated has been carried to its full term, we shall be in possession of a system of rules, by which the criticism of the technical part at least of lyrical poetry may be reduced to the form of propositions capable of being logically argued and debated, and entirely removed from that indefinite region of taste which, like the so-called discretion of a judge, does not admit of being made the subject of rational discussion.

provide for the easy transmission and flow of breath (unless a suspension is desired for some cause, or is unavoidable) from one into the other.

The great topic of Phonetic Syzygy has something in common with each of these flanking principles. In matter it agrees with Symptosis, in form (in respect of operating with distinct reference to continuity of impression) it borders upon Anastomosis.

We look to Metric for correctness of form, to Chromatic for beauty of color; it is to Synectic, and to its main branch Syzygy, that we must attend in order to secure that coherence, compactness, and ring of true metal, without which no versification deserves the name of poetry. It is to Syzygy that I have called most attention in my annotations, and it was with this principle exclusively that at the outset I intended to deal. The subject has grown upon me in passing through the press; and the book has been built up in a most unforeseen and unpremeditated manner, which I state in order to account for the numerous dislocations, ill-fittings, gaps and other irregularities of structure, as well as occasional repetitions, which I must beg the courteous reader to overlook or excuse. In fact the work may be truly said to have been born, cradled, and nurtured in the press, nay often to have fallen asleep there, to awake like a *baby refreshed*, hungry and calling for more. I began with a single fly-leaf containing a translation of 'Tyrrhena Regum' for distribution among the audience at the Penny Reading where I was to recite the ode. This, doubled subsequently into a half-sheet, augmented with notes, assimilating to itself fresh matter, and leading me off into unintended analyses and discussions, has grown up by successive stages and additions into its present form, the simulacrum of a full-fledged book—to the surprise of no one so much as that of the originator of its being.

In my translations from Horace, especially in the first of them, I have aimed at a high ideal of fidelity to the original—probably at a higher one than has been achieved or even attempted in Metre since the days of Milton. What success has attended this effort, philologically speaking, I must leave to others to determine; but I can speak with some confidence as to the agreeable musical impression made on audiences illiterate as well as literate by its recital, and may do so without violation of modesty, as an evidence of the scientific correctness of my principles of versificatory construction.* The great law of

* Starting from the safe postulate, that Horace's ear was as

Continuity (continuity of sound and continuity of mental impression) has been my guiding star throughout. Some of my readers may chance to remember that I laid much stress upon this principle in the inaugural address delivered by me as President of the Mathematical and Physical Section of the British Association for the Advancement of Science, at Exeter. I went, on that occasion, so far as to say that Mathematics under its existent aspect might be defined as the Science of Continuity. I have thought, then, that this would be a not unsuitable occasion for republishing the address in a separate form, as I have received frequent applications for copies of it, with which I have not had the means of complying.

The address in an abridged form, under the title, ' A Plea for the Mathematician,' was published by request of the Editor of *Nature* in two numbers of that valuable journal, with additional notes, which are here reproduced. In an appendix will be found the letters of a correspondence which grew out of these notes, concerning the improper description of Kant's doctrine of Time and Space, common with Scotch and English writers on

---

perfect as his taste is irreproachable, I have been able to apply syzygetic principles in aid of settling two disputed readings in the Latin text of 'Tyrrhena Regum,' (*Od.* iii. 3, 29,) lines 6 and 34.

Mental Science. This very mischievous locution, which although countenanced by the practice of some of our best authors, suggests a view of Kant's doctrine diametrically opposed to its most characteristic feature, and that which differentiates it from all preceding systems of Philosophy, it is believed has hereby received its death-blow, and must henceforth disappear from the face of English literature.

P.S.—In the prefatory letter to the volume of collected 'Lay Sermons, Addresses, and Reviews,' with which Professor Huxley has recently gratified the public, I notice some remarks which he has made on the inaugural address above referred to. He says, addressing himself to Dr. Tyndall: ' In the same paper (On the Educational Value of the Natural History Sciences) there is a statement concerning the method of the mathematical sciences, which repeated and expanded elsewhere brought upon me, during the meeting of the British Association at Exeter, the artillery of our eminent friend Professor Sylvester.

' No one knows better than you do, how readily I should defer to the opinion of so great a mathematician if the question at issue were really, as he seems to think it is, a mathematical one. But

I submit, that the dictum of a mathematical athlete upon a difficult problem which mathematics offer to philosophy, has no more special weight than the verdict of that great pedestrian Captain Barclay would have had in settling a disputed point in the physiology of locomotion.'

To this I need only reply that I am not aware what reason Professor Huxley has for attributing to me the opinion that it is a mathematical question to determine the place of mathematics among the sciences. I have only ventured to express my belief that had the distinguished lay preacher been better acquainted with the real aim and scope of mathematics he would scarcely have committed himself to saying that the teaching of languages is of the same general nature as 'mathematical training.' I remain of that belief still. Supposing that Professor Huxley had had no acquaintance with the anatomy, physiology, and habits of the human subject, would he have felt himself justified in writing as he has done, 'On the Place of Man in Nature;' or, supposing he had done so, would what he wrote have been likely to achieve the world-wide celebrity of his actual work on the subject?*

* I may possibly have misquoted the title. I remember seeing a translation into German of the book I mean, lying on the counter of an Italian bookseller in Florence.

He further adds, 'The genius which sighs for new worlds to conquer beyond that surprising region in which "geometry, algebra, and the theory of numbers melt into one another like sunset tints, or the colours of a dying dolphin," may be of comparatively little service in the cold domain (mostly lighted by the moon, some say) of philosophy. And the more I think of it, the more does our friend seem to me to fall into the position of one of those " verständige Leute," about whom he makes so apt a quotation from Goethe. Surely he has not duly considered two points. The first, that I am in no way answerable for the origination of the doctrine he criticises: and the second, that if we are to employ the terms observation, induction, and experiment, in the sense in which he uses them, logic is as much an observational, inductive, and experimental science as mathematics; and that, I confess, appears to me to be a *reductio ad absurdum* of his argument.'

With regard to the first of 'the two points' here raised, I would say that Professor Huxley, whether or not answerable for the origination, is certainly answerable for the vindication and propagation, with 'repetition and expansion,' of the erroneous doctrine which formed the subject of my criticism. I felt no call to go into so purely subjective a question as that of ascertaining the sources from which he had drawn the erroneous opinions which found in him their advocate.

As regards the second of the two points I am perfectly at a loss to understand how Professor Huxley can suppose that the observational, inductive, and experimental processes which I have referred to and illustrated in their bearing on the illimitable sphere of mathematical discovery and invention, can be shown to have any place in the confined and circumscribed area of pure logic. In a word, without the slightest intention of saying anything unkind or discourteous, I cannot conceal my opinion that what my estimable and eminent adversary calls a *reductio ad absurdum* might with much greater propriety be termed a *deductio ex absurdo:* for it seems to me absurd to suppose that there exists in the science of pure logic anything that bears a resemblance to the infinitely developable and interminable euristic processes of mathematical science.

J. J. S.

ATHENAEUM CLUB,
   July, 1870.

CONTENTS.

Laws of Verse, or Principles of Versification, exemplified in Metrical Translations.

                                              PAGE

I. TRANSLATION OF HOR. OD. iii. 29.
    Exhibition of perduntistic or dichotomous plan   .   25
    Original   26–28
    Translation   27–31
    Notes   30–41
    Criticism of Conington's Version   42
    Function of Ryme in Verse   44
    Laws of Anastomosis and Syzygy   45
    The Alcaic Stanza formulated   47
    Evidence of Horace's native Mathematical Power .   48
Poeta fit, non nascitur   49
II. SCHILLER—'Die Ideale'   49
    Theory of the Diphthong   50
III. UHLAND—'Des Goldschmieds Töchterlein' .   53
IV. SCHILLER—'Cassandra'   56
    Theory of Alliteration . . . . .   ib.
V. GOETHE—'Trost in Thränen' . . .   62
    Formation of the feminine transcendental pluperfect superlative adjective   63
    Synectic, the Author's right-of-way into the Realm of Rhythm   64
    'Synectic' explained . . . . .   ib.
    Concerning modern Metric and accentual Feet .   65
    Metre in terms of Music   66

		PAGE
	Rhythmical rests	67
	Metric Criticism of opening lines of 'Bride of Abydos,' &c.	ib.
	Imaginary Rhythmical time	69
	Success of experimental Recital of Example I.	70
VI.	Hor. Od. III. 29—Earlier Version	71
VII.	Schiller—'An den Frühling'	74
VIII.	Blumauer—'An die Donau'	75
	Spontaneous Generation of the present Version	ib.
IX.	Uhland—'Der Wirthin Töchterlein'	76
X.	Rückert—'Die Locke der Begrabenen'	77
XI.	Uhland—'Das Schloss am Meere'	79
	Syzygetic Key	81

ANONYMOUS POEMS.

XII.	The Evening Star	81
XIII.	Acrostic	82
XIV.	Winter	ib.
XV.	To an Ink-spot upon a Lady's cheek	83
XVI.	Melancholy	ib.
XVII.	April 30	85
XVIII.	Indifference	86
XIX.	Remonstrance	87
XX.	Faith	88
XXI.	Kepler's Apostrophe	89
XXII.	'Occhi! stelle immortali'	91
XXIII.	What's in a Name?	ib.
XXIV.	Hor. Od. III. xxvii. 25.—The Story of Europa	93
	Notes—*Medias fraudes*: its twelve meanings	95
	Virgineum culpæ and Professor Newman	96
	Nomina: transcendental significance of the plural form	97

Inaugural Address to the Mathematical and Physical Section of the British Association, at Exeter, August, 1869.

	PAGE
Introductory Remarks	101
Vindication of the mathematician as man—'Homo mathematicus'	105
Professor Huxley's opinions on mathematical science—his parallel of grammatical and mathematical training	106
Mathematics as dependent on invention and observation—Examples of mathematical euristic	108
Contact-points of faith and knowledge in mathematics	114
Mathematical discovery dependent on observation of mathematical phenomena	115
The theory of reducible cyclodes	117
The place of physical science relative to mathematics	119
Healthful effect of mathematical meditation on mind and body—Dii majores of the mathematical Pantheon	121
Mental and spiritual gratification furnished by mathematics	123
Mathematics the science of continuity	125
Examples of mathematical relations	127
Concluding remarks	129
Postscript—Letter from Dr. Jacobi	ib.

APPENDIX.

On the Incorrect Description of Kant's Doctrine of Space and Time common in English writers.

Correspondence on the part of:
G. H. Lewes	131
T. H. Huxley	132

C. M. Ingleby	133
J. J. Sylvester	ib.
G. H. Lewes	134
G. Croom Robertson	138
W. H. Stanley Monck	ib.
J. J. Sylvester	140
George Henry Lewes	143
W. H. Stanley Monck	146
Catena of passages from the foregoing correspondence bearing on Mr. Lewes' final letter	148
Illustration of author's position drawn from Mr. Herbert Spencer's supposed refutation of Kant	151

LAWS OF VERSE.

ERRATA.

Page	line	for	read
9	11	*Poetica*	*poetica*.
10	2	principal branches	principal sections.
21	23	*dele* adjective.	
23	16	*dele from* Healthful *to* body.	
37	29 (end of 2nd par.) page 1	page 25.
47	7	or as, say,	or as we say.
59, note, line 6, *dele the second* besides.			
73	7	smoke	smooth.
80	11	sigh	dirge.
98	24	56.]	26.]
150	11	*read* (γ) So far from averring that the former ' (form *of* understanding) ' is " indefensible," it is what I declare to be true.'	

And in like manner each of the eight duads above may be rendered into separate stanzas containing a single and distinct subject or image. It would of course be easy, and not uninstructive, to arrange this paradigm under the form of a tree bearing two stems, four branches, eight branchlets, and sixteen twigs or terminals.

LAWS OF VERSE,

on,

Principles of Versification,

EXEMPLIFIED IN METRICAL TRANSLATIONS.

I. TRANSLATION OF HOR. OD. III. 29.

Originally printed for Recital and Distribution at a Penny Reading held in the National School Rooms, Eltham, December 22, 1869.

EXHIBITION OF THE PERDUALISTIC OR DICHOTOMOUS PLAN OF THE CONSTRUCTION OF HOR. CAR. III. 29.

1—16 The ODE.

1—8 Extroitive.	9—16 Introitive.
1—4 Invitation.	9—12 Impersonal.
5—8 Exhortation.	13—16 Personal.
1—2 Come into the country.	9—10 Life like a river.
3—4 Leave Rome.	11—12 The past indefeasible.
5—6 The season favours.	13—14 He defies fortune.
7—8 Throw aside care.	15—16 He has nothing to lose.

[*The numbers refer to the order of the stanzas.*]

And in like manner each of the eight duads above may be rendered into separate stanzas containing a single and distinct subject or image. It would of course be easy, and not uninstructive, to arrange this paradigm under the form of a tree bearing two stems, four branches, eight branchlets, and sixteen twigs or terminals.

B

Q. HORATII FLACCI CARMINUM
III. 29.

AD MAECENATEM.

Tyrrhena regum progenies, tibi
Non ante verso lene merum cado,
   Cum flore, Maecenas, rosarum, et
      Pressa tuis balanus capillis

Jamdudum apud me est. Eripe te morae: [v.
Ne semper udum Tibur, et Aefulae
   Declive contempleris arvum, et
      Telegoni juga parricidae.

Fastidiosam desere copiam et   [ix.
Molem propinquam nubibus arduis:
   Omitte mirari beatae
      Fumum et opes strepitumque Romae.

Plerumque gratae divitibus vices,   [xiii.
Mundaeque parvo sub lare pauperum
   Coenae, sine aulaeis et ostro,
      Sollicitam explicuere frontem.

Jam clarus occultum Andromedae pater   [xvii.
Ostendit ignem: jam Procyon furit
   Et stella vesani Leonis,
      Sole dies referente siccos.

AN ODE OF HORACE.
III. 29.

To Maecenas.

Birth of Tyrrhenian regal line !
In unstooped cask, a mellow brew
Roses and myrrh those locks of thine
Fresh pressed Maecenas ! to bedew,

Long wait thee here ! Shake off delay,   [5
Nor spray-washed Tibur still gaze on
Nor Aefule's slope, nor heights survey
Of parricidal Telegon.

Quit gorged Profusion, and the pile   [9
That soars to loftiest clouds akin ;
Pause in admiring for awhile,
Thrice-happy Rome's, smoke, traffic, din.

Ofttimes the rich love change ; walls bare   [13
And trim meals lacking purple woof
Have smoothed their wrinkled brow of care,
'Neath many a poor man's lowly roof.

Now Andromede's bright Sire doth show   [17
Light erewhile hid : now Procyon's rays
Flash, and mad Leo's, as below
The Sun draws back dry summer days.

Jam pastor umbras cum grege languido   [xxi.
Rivumque fessus quaerit, et horridi
   Dumeta Silvani: caretque
     Ripa vagis taciturna ventis.

Tu civitatem quis deceat statue   [xxv.
Curas, et Urbi sollicitus times,
   Quid Seres et regnata Cyro
     Bactra parent Tanaisque discors.

Prudens futuri temporis exitum   [xxix.
Caliginosa nocte premit Deus,
   Ridetque, si mortalis ultra
     Fas trepidat. Quod adest memento

Componere aequus: cetera fluminis   [xxxiii.
Ritu feruntur, nunc medio alveo
   Cum pace delabentis Etruscum
     In mare, nunc lapides adesos,

Stirpesque raptas, et pecus et domos   [xxxvii.
Volventis una, non sine montium
   Clamore vicinaeque silvae,
     Quum fera diluvies quietos

Irritat amnes. Ille potens sui   [xli.
Laetusque deget, cui licet in diem
   Dixisse, ' Vixi: cras vel atra
     Nube polum Pater occupato

' Vel sole puro: non tamen irritum,   [xlv.
Quodcunque retro est, efficiet: neque
   Diffinget infectumque reddet,
     Quod fugiens semel hora vexit.'

Now with spent flock tired shepherds hie [21
To shades and brook and thickets dank
Of Silvan hoar: and stray winds die
And all lies hushed, upon the bank.

Thou heed'st what form the State beseems, [25
And watchful fear'st for Rome from far
What Ind or realm of Cyrus schemes,
Bactria or Tanais rent with war.

Farseeing God in murkiest night [29
Enshrouds of future years the goal,
And smiles if Man in fate's despite
Frets his brief hour: With steadfast soul

Set right the present! all besides [33
Doth onwards like the River flow,
That now in smooth mid-channel glides
To join Etruria's sea below;

Now when fierce floods stir its dull rills, [37
With trunks upwrenched and waveworn stone,
Midst roar of neighbouring woods and hills,
Flocks, herds, and houses, whirls in one.

Lord of Himself and blest shall prove, [41
He who can boast from day to day,
'I've lived: to-morrow let high Jove
Black cloud or sunshine, as he may,

'Pour o'er the Pole! what's come and gone [45
To frustrate, doth defy his power;
Or aught to unshape or make undone,
Once ravished by the flying hour.'

30 Principles of Versification exemplified.

Fortuna sævo laeta negotio, et [XLIX.
Ludum insolentem ludere pertinax,
 Transmutat incertos honores,
  Nunc mihi, nunc alii benigna.

Laudo manentem : si celeres quatit [LIII.
Pennas, resigno quae dedit, et mea
 Virtute me involvo, probamque
  Pauperiem sine dote quaero.

Non est meum, si mugiat Africis [LVII.
Malus procellis, ad miseras preces
 Decurrere ; et votis pacisci,
  Ne Cypriae Tyriaeve merces

Addant avaro divitias mari. [LXI.
Tum me, biremis praesidio scaphae
 Tutum, per Aegaeos tumultus
  Aura feret geminusque Pollux.

NOTES.

1.] I propose as an alternative rendering what follows below :—

   Tyrrhenian progeny of kings!
   In unstooped cask a mellow brew
   Roses and balm-drawn myrrh-droppings
   Thy hair Maecenas to bedew.

I hesitated, and chopped and changed a long time, as my printers can too well attest, between the two readings, 'Birth of Tyrrhenian' and 'Tyrrhenian, birth of'; and yet it is as certain as any proposition in Euclid can be that the former is the proper order of the words. The latter, it is true, has in its favour a closer correspondence with the original, and the fact of the initial T being a crisper and grander opening sound than the B; but this

Fortune at work with savage glee [49
On mocking game, remorseless bent,
Shifts her light favors, now to me,
To another now, beneficent.

I greet her stay: but if anew [53
She shakes swift wings, her gifts abjure
And wrapped in my own virtue woo
Poverty, portionless but pure.

Not mine, if straining topmasts roar [57
'Neath Afric's storms, with piteous prayers
Or bargaining vows each God to implore,
Lest Cyprus' or fine Tyrian wares

Add treasure to the ravening seas! [61
Me then, upborne on pair-oared craft,
Shall twin-lit Pollux and the breeze,
Safe through the tossed Aegean, waft.

---

cannot outweigh the double objection,—1st, of the *b* in 'birth' following the *n* in 'Tyrrhenian,' contrary to the laws of Anastomosis; and, 2nd, of the number and measure of 'Tyrrha' being to the number and measure of 'Tyrrhenian birth of re,' as 1:3; whereas, in the contrary order, the corresponding ratio is as 2:3, —which latter, by the principles of Symptosis (here applying to the clash or congruence of the open *ē* sounds) is preferable, especially at the opening of the piece, as being less suggestive of subdivision of measure. I use the word clash here in no bad sense (for which the word jar or *jangle* may be reserved), but to signify generally the relation between two sounds strongly recalling each other, which may be agreeable or offensive (scarcely ever neutral) according to the circumstances in which it occurs. When agreeable, for want of a better term, a clash may provisionally be styled a *congruence*, when offensive, a *jar*. Thus, ex. gr., rhymes and alliterations (properly employed) are of the nature of *clashes*. It is worth noticing, that a similar struggle for survivorship of the fittest occurs in the second line of my version. On syncetic (syzygetic) grounds, 'stirred' (by virtue of its stirring r's) would be preferable to 'stooped,' but the latter word, besides expressing the precise action of bending down the cask to get the liquor out of it, is chromatically preferable, by virtue of the colorific (and also slightly syzygetic) value of its pure vowel sound. Moreover, the *p* in 'stoop-ed' has a fair syzygetic value as corroborative of the *B* in birth, and precursory to the *p* in 'pressed,' which itself *preconises* and ushers in a well-sustained and glittering p syzygy in the two succeeding stanzas.

III.] I do not know what authority Forcellini has for interpreting *verso* to mean *turned* or *tilted up*. I think I have seen *amphorae* in a cellar to one of the houses in Pompeii, the natural way of bringing which out for use would be by *turning them round* in contact with the wall against which they lean. Conington and Newman by their renderings of *Non ante verso*, 'unbroached,' 'unop'd,' appear to adopt Forcellini's explanation, and are of course much more likely to be right than I am—if they have sufficiently weighed the point.*

IV.] A sly hit at Maecenas' notorious foible for hair-washes.

4.] See Suetonius, *Aug.* 86, referred to in Smith's 'Classical Dictionary' (art. Maecenas), and note the word μυροβρεχείς applied by Augustus to Maecenas' *cincinnos*.

VI.] I believe the application of *semper* to *udum* or *contempleris* to have been consciously left ambiguous by the Poet. A similar remark applies to *plerumque*, and to the construction of the whole of the first line of the 4th stanza. This kind of ambiguity or amphibolism is no blemish, but, on the contrary, a source of gain as giving greater fulness to the conception: the mind seizes upon the same word successively in different connections without *pausing* to decide upon which is intended, so that there is no interruption of continuity, the one irremissible sin of lyrical composition, the sole purpose of which is, through the ear and the intellect, twin channels of the soul, to bring the hearer into emotional sympathy with the composer. Conington's rendering of *semper-udum* by *never dried* seems to me singularly infelicitous: an *undried*

---

* Since the above was in print, Professor Key has kindly furnished me with a passage from Plautus' 'Stichus,' v. 4. 39, which he reads, 'Namque etiepol quam inde subito vel cadus versi potest!' which serves to settle the question, and proves that the common rendering of *verso* is correct.

plain, besides being an unusual form of speech, suggests rather the idea of rheumatism and dampness than that of freshness and coolness, which was evidently in the poet's mind.

VIII.] The three places named would be seen in succession (in a sort of irregular arc of a circle) from Mæcenas' Belvedere, as he turned his gaze *further and further away* from Horace's farm: an ethical and geographical refutation (if any were needed) of the gratuitous substitution (adopted by Anthon, and Tate before him, and mentioned without reprobation by Conington) of *Ut* for *Ne* in the 6th line. I abstain from referring to the cacophony of this preposterous misreading, and the pernicious rupture of the resumption (after the usual agreeable break in a single fourth line) of the beautiful syzygy of *s* sounds. One mischief attending the introduction of printing is the depravation of the phonetic judgment of verse consequent upon the appeal being transferred from the ear to the eye. To request a friend to turn his back upon the place of one's abode would be a very Irish way of inviting him to pay a visit to his (the inviter's) part of the country. Any who object to the bifid rendering of CONTRAHES may substitute *so* for *still* in 6 and *alway* for *survey* in 8.

IX.] The continuity of sense makes it, I think, natural to understand *copia* as referring to some (I do not say what) *form of contrast*, as, ex. gr., the tiresome extent of the Rue de Rivoli or the interminable Champs Elysées in Paris. Plenty, abundance, or luxury appears to me rather incongruous with what immediately follows. I felt half inclined, upon a sort of *cy-pris* principle (taking sound and sense into simultaneous account), to substitute *loathed profusion* for *palling plenty*.*

* Since the above was in print, I became unable to resist the phonetic seduction of the words 'loathed profusion,' which are so advantageous as regards time, melody, and imitative effect, and accordingly incorporated them in the text. I believe *fastidiosam* admits of two principal meanings—that which conceives disgust, i.e. nice, delicate, squeamish, fastidious; and that which produces disgust. The former meaning in this connection would imply a personification of *copia*, which does not seem quite suited to the context; and between causing loathing and being loathed the difference is not so very wide. Whilst in the act of meditating on the sound and meaning of the words *fastidiosam copiam*, a splendid Yorkshire pie, the gift of a kind and generous friend in the North, was placed upon my luncheon table, and the meaning of the words in a moment became clear; for the fulness of the contents occasioned in me such a *sympathetic sense of repletion*, that I was unable to touch a mouthful, and finally quartered it out untasted among my friends and neighbours, by whom it was gratefully appreciated. I felt, too, at the same time, how well the unctuous, spongaceous sound of the words

34 *Principles of Versification exemplified.*

XII.] I have no doubt that *opes* is intended to conjure up the image of piled-up wares and waggon-loads choking up the thoroughfares, and would unhesitatingly have translated it by *glut* were it not that that word could only be carried off by a change of form in the verse and translating *beatas* as *glittering*, which, although partially justified by Orelli's paraphrase *opulenta ac splendida*, I felt would be flying off too wide from the text, to venture on. Smoky, *busy*, noisy Rome is evidently what is intended: the very identical epithets that I lately saw applied to London in some penny newspaper.

12.] The common rendering of *opes* and *beatae* makes *beatas* redundant and reduces *opes* to the position of a tame elephant between two wild ones. It must be, I think, clear to any unprejudiced mind that *beatas* is simply ironical or sub-ironical, and '*fumum et opes strepitumque*' a phrase of collective disparagement.

15.] For sound and poetical effect, I should of course prefer '*the*' to '*their* wrinkled brow of care,' but it seems imperative to preserve the distinct antithesis between *divitibus* and *pauperum*, which disappears in Conington's and other of the current renderings.

16.] The reciter will please pronounce the *c* hard like *k*, for the sake of supporting the final sound of *back* in the 4th line. Notice too in l. 5, *ante*, how the initial word of this line, besides touching up the colour in *off* in the same line, lends a very sensible support to the final word in the line following.

23.] I believe *horridus* in English public schools is usually translated *prickly*, which appears rather unmeaning. I suspect that in some way or another it must refer to the particular state of the woods at the time of year in question. In my state of ignorance as to its exact signification I have deemed it permissible to translate the word according to sound and blind association (not disdainful even of that suggested by the *prickly* hoar-frost) instead of sense.

XXIII.] Dryden, in his admirable free version, which he says

(tolerably well preserved, I think, in the translation) corresponded to the sense of cloying and satiness engendered by the closely-packed and luscious contents of the spacious walls of the party. Those who please may read *palling plenty*, *palling luxury*, or *cloying plenty*, or *dull repletion*, in lieu of *loathed profusion*. But finally I have made up my mind since the above was set up in print that it is better to accept a personification of copia (for which there is no lack of precedent) and to substitute *gorged* for *loathed* as having idealistic, quantitative, chromatic, and syzygetic reasons in its favour which collectively far outweigh a trifling inferiority to *loathed* in point of assonemials.

'he has taken some pains to make his masterpiece in English,' and which we are told Mr. Fox declared to be superior to the original (*vide* Lowell's Six Essays), takes a strange liberty with the word *Silvani*, and upon the strength of it invents the line—
'The Sylvans to their shades retire.'

Who were these Sylvans, one would like to know. Oddly enough, Francis, following suit, gives—

'While rustic Sylvans seek the glade'

as the equivalent for *horridi dumeta Silvani*. This Dryden's self-acknowledged masterpiece is not included in the plan of Mr. Christie's very clever edition of Dryden. In Scott's edition (the second is the one I have seen) the editor has been careless enough to refer persistently to the ode as the 29th of the FIRST book. It is certainly a pity that so magnificent and Rubens-like a canvas should be spoiled by occasional instances of bad taste (which might as easily have been avoided or corrected), such as the daub of the Sylvans just adverted to, and 'The new Lord Mayor'! corresponding to *Tu civitatem quis decent status*, in the 7th stanza of the original. Imagine Milton committing such a barbarism! The higher civilization of England must for a time have been submerged after the restoration of the hateful Stuarts. Mr. Lowell (if I remember aright) expresses surprise that Dryden should feel so strongly and so repeatedly give vent to his sense of freedom and unshackledness when having ten syllables in a line to deal with instead of eight. I am more surprised that Mr. Lowell, who is said to write excellent poetry himself, should be surprised by anything of the kind. To me the difference between the two seems like that between bathing in a pond or inland creek as compared with a plunge in the open sea: the very *embarras de choix*, the sense of infinite variety of combination and unlimited room for disporting the imagination at will has deterred me from more than timidly venturing upon this form of verse, as a miniature-painter would naturally shrink from trying his pencil on a historical canvas. Between octosyllabic and dekasyllabic verse, the interval is as wide as between playing at marbles and bowls, or as between bagatelle and billiards. If we calculate on an average two syllables to a word (and as the true average is less, this is much understating my own argument), we have five words in a line in one case against four in the other, which by the theory of permutations gives a

36 *Principles of Versification exemplified.*

facility as 120 to 24, i.e. as 5 to 1. Or, again, let us look to the variety of form (so strangely neglected by all writers on versification), but so very important an element of the general effect, which depends on the manner in which syllables are combined into words or into word-groups, i.e. groups which read like single words. According to the theory of partitions (this being a case of partition whose permutations count as distinct), the number of forms of groupings for x syllables is 2^x; accordingly, the advantage in dealing with 10 as compared with 8 syllables is as 1,024 to 256, i.e. as 4 to 1. Hence we see that the magnified facility of decasyllabic over octosyllabic verse is not, as at a superficial glance one might suppose, as 5 to 4, but as at the very least 5 or 4 to 1. Writers like Conington or Newman have noticed the extreme case of monosyllabic lines, but no one seems to have drawn especial attention to the distinct character and aspect attaching to every different form of syllable groupings in a line. The working out of this theory belongs to the subject of *rests*, there being an incalculably small but still perfectly sensible interruption of breathing between every two groups of syllables; the doctrine of caesura and of line-stops is the very self-same theory extended to the case of compound groups. I may notice as the result of a careful and tolerably extensive induction that an octosyllabic quatrain (which might, arithmetically speaking, consist of 32 simple groups), if it contain more than 24 will, in general, be found defective in *tension:* 21 or 22 may be reckoned as high concert pitch. As another useful piece of statistical information I may mention here, that for the purpose of easy but not diffuse rendering from Latin into English, the number of English should be to the number of Latin syllables, in a ratio intermediate to $\frac{3}{4}$ and $\frac{5}{6}$. I of course suppose that the number of lines is maintained the same in the original and translation, i.e. that the rendering is line for line, although not necessarily line into line.

24.] The comma in this line is inserted to indicate that a slight pause should be introduced to give effect to the word *hush*. The fact is one wants a double system of punctuation in verse— one to indicate the grammatical construction, and another the emissions of breath; and in default of this, it becomes necessary to lean, sometimes to one principle and sometimes to the other, in following the actual system.*

* A friend informs me that an edition of the New Testament (very hard to procure) has been printed with rhetorical pauses, and I have lately seen

28.] Notice the *tr* and *tn* of the first and third words collected in *inverted* order in the word *rent*. Contrast the effect of *rent* with its equivalent in *sense form*, where the *system of sounds* is left unclosed. So, too, I have taken a slight liberty with the text in substituting 'Bactria' for 'Bactra,' for the sake of the opposition of the *ia* in the former to *ai* in 'Tanais,' as well as to avoid the necessity of a musical *rest* after the first word of the line.

XXXII.] The entire Ode is constructed (consciously, I believe, by the Poet) on a dualistic, or, to speak more precisely, a perdualistic principle. The *catena* in the text is purposely inserted by Horace to ease off the transition between the superincumbent and subjacent main divisions—the body of the coach and the carriage proper, so to say—(8 stanzas to each); and is bound to be maintained by a translator true to his author at any and every cost. There are five principal species of *catenae*, or rivets, as they might be termed : the simple, the duplex, the prolate, the oblate, and the agglutinate, of each of which there are instances in this Ode. By *perdualistic* I mean that the 16 stanzas subdivide into two natural ideological groups of 8 each, each of these octads into two of 4 each, and so on until we arrive at single stanzas. It has been pointed out to me by a lady of high culture that in the 'Vita Nuova' Dante explains the distribution of each sonnet (according to the Ideas) into a definite number of component parts ; but what is especially noticeable in this Ode is the continued dichotomy or bifurcation, springing from one fundamental root-idea, carried out (consistently with the poet's passion for exactness) upon a principle of strict arithmetical precision. A paradigm of the deduction is given at page 1.

34.] The word Etruscum in the third line demonstrates that the Poet, poet-like, had a particular river in his mind's eye. My friend Dr. Ingleby suggests the Tiber, in which I have no doubt he is right; and to him I am indebted for the introduction of the capital R in River. In Bunsen's 'Life,' by his widow, I think I remember reading of a Miss Bathurst who was drowned when riding by the banks of the Tiber, in consequence of a sudden rise in the river. I remember too, many years ago,

advertised Charles Kemble's readings from Shakspear on a somewhat similar plan. Blank spaces left between words might be used to indicate the relative durations of pauses (or in some cases mere slowness of articulation), desiderated by the composer.

travelling by diligence on the coast road between Valencia (of the Cid) and Barcelona, and passing, not very far from the latter city, a spot as dry and seemingly as little liable to inundation as the Ladies' Mile in the Park, where only a week before, the diligence, by the sudden descent of a mountain torrent, had been swept into the sea. I was told that the passengers (including two young Englishmen out on a vacation tour) were all drowned with the exception of a Civil Guard, one of two who had got up into the diligence just before the catastrophe occurred.

29.] Orelli's authority, and Anthon's (who, I suppose, is good enough as a sounding-board for collecting and reverberating opinions), justify me, I trust, in associating the idea of fate with the words *ultra fas*, although I believe such interpretation runs counter to the current English public school tradition. *Mortalis*, I presume, is intended, or at least serves in the original to suggest the notion of the brevity of life, which I indicate by 'brief hour.' *Trepidat*, Professor Key tells me, is connected with the word τρέω, and with the notion of turning one's head up and down, round and about, in a state of nervous anxiety. Professor Newman translates it 'strains his nerves' (!). The English school-boy or competitive-examination word *funk* seems to me to come nearest to it in meaning, and, like *trepidat*, is used generally in an intransitive, but occasionally in an active, sense.

XXXIV.] It seems to me certain, on *phonetic* grounds, that *alveo*, and not *aequore*, is the true reading. 1st. Having regard to the jingle of *aequus* with *aequore*. 2nd. On the score of the pernicious interruption of the beautiful *l* syzygy if the latter reading be adopted. Since the above was in print, I am happy to find this opinion sanctioned, on quite distinct grounds, by the transcendent authority of my friend Professor Key: 'The story is so improbable that it must be true, for no one would have thought of inventing it.' This is the sole sort of argument brought forward in defence of the 'aequore' reading, which Orelli does not seem to have shown his usual good judgment in retaining.

XLI.] Evidently *amnes* are the rills feeding the *flumen*. I have seen somewhere a reference to the former word used in conjunction with *lebetis*. The two stanzas (9th and 10th) lie double-locked and, as it were, screwed together between rivets fore and aft, and are manifestly intended to be welded into a unity of the closest kind.

XLIV.] Pater = Diespiter = Sky Jove = High Jove; *pater* is precisely the right word to employ in connexion with skyey influences, and 'High' (sitting up above) is its true English equivalent.

46.] A very esteemed friend strongly objects to the phrase 'Pour o'er the pole!' and informs me that he is in the habit, when he recites my verses, of substituting *sky* for *pole*. This may be better for distinctness of sense, but it is defective in point of syzygy, and I advisedly adhere to the reading in the text, the sound of which, I think, imitates the effect of sunshine gradually diffusing itself over the zenith.

49.] The sounds of the concluding word in this stanza would be ineffably weak were they not supported upon the principle of accumulation by being struck in the preceding lines. The ear is a great integrator. Sounds linger and declare their affinities in the ear long after the words to which they belong have disappeared from the memory. I was once much puzzled to account for the disagreeable effect produced by the use of the word 'Leave' (now 'Quit') for *desere* in the 9th line of this version, and it was some time before I discovered that it was owing to the word 'rose-leaves' (now 'Roses') having been used by me in the 3rd line.

51.] I am perfectly satisfied that *honores* here means *marks of personal regard* (i. e. favors) of Fortune as a *woman*, in the same way as *decernere honores* means *to decree marks of public regard*. It is only by an accidental coincidence that *honores* in this place includes the notion of our English word *honors* along with *health*, *wealth*, *success*, etc., the value of Fortune's *favors* in current coin. Conington, almost always judicious in interpretation, has apparently taken the same view, and translates *honores* by 'caresses,' which is, I think, going too far, although in the right direction. Professor Newman, on the other hand, gives an unmeaning verbal rendering, 'uncertain glories.'

52.] The intention of this rendering is to redintegrate the unity of the original stanza, the four assertions contained in which I understand as referring to the single image of Fortune cheating at some sort of thimble-rigging game, which has possibly come down to us from prehistoric times—it would sound better, but be inaccurate, for me to speak of our Aryan ancestors. After all the pains taken, this stanza still remains the least satisfactory of the lot. I made and broke upwards of two hundred distinct castings of the stanza before I could satisfy myself that the requisite idealistic conditions were fairly complied with, and I believe that a solution of the difficulty would have been impossible but for the artifice of carrying back to an antecedent line the sense of *Nunc mihi*. A guinea a line, if one takes the necessary pains to work up one's verses to an approximately equal pitch and polish, is often poor pay enough, when breakage is taken into account, as is done in estimating the cost of grinding large object-glasses for telescopes. Does any stanza in this Ode ever present more than a single *tableau* or scheme of related ideas?

LIII. Lord Lytton credits Orelli with a reference to a coin containing an effigy of Fortune in a sitting posture, and an inscription, 'Fortunae Manenti.' The same reference is given at length in the old Delphin.

LV.] See Forcellini for examples of *antithesis* in one and the same sentence between *virtus* and *probitas*—the fortitude and courage of man, as opposed to the chastity and purity of woman. It seems a work of supererogation to add that *virtus* can have nothing to do with the Christian notion of virtue, or with the use of the word in the passage cited as a parallel one by Mr. Theodore Martin:—

> 'And evermore himself with comfort feeds
> Of his own virtues and praiseworthy deeds.'

The parallelism, so far as I can see, consists merely in the two passages not having, nor being capable of being produced on either side to have, a single point in common.

56.] This stanza may, at the reader's discretion, be replaced by the following one:—

> 'Welcome to stay! but if she shake
> Swift wings her bounties I resign,
> And wrapped in my own virtue make
> Pure Poverty unportioned mine.'

Welcome to stay! anticipatory of Conington's 'Stays she? 'tis well,' appeared in my original version, and is more idiomatic and slightly more true to the sense of the original than 'I greet her stay.' *Resign* is better than *abjure*, and the interpolation *anew* is well got rid of. The objection to the new version is the weakness of the ending of the third line and the substitution of wedding for wooing. A learned and witty friend, it is true, has sought to quiet my scruples on this last head by suggesting that the consent of *Pauperies*, however *proba*, might be assumed to a reasonably good offer; but 'a philosopher in his thin dress of virtue clad' would, I trow, hardly justify such a designation.

The repetition of *mine* in the first line of the following stanza, if a fault, which it is not, but rather the contrary, to my ears (and is, I am told, justified by precedent in Edgar Poe, where that form of repetition is used as a source of embellishment) could be obviated by reading 'Not I when' for 'Not mine if,' and 'implore' for 'to implore.' I believe the determining cause in my mind for keeping the stanza as it stands in the text is that the fourth line has been honoured by the approval of an eminent poet, whose instructions (in such a matter, commands) to me were not on any account to change it. Such approval converts the line into a 'pearl of price,' which it would be folly and unthrift to let go. The third line, too, in the same quatrain has equally met with the approval of a great Cambridge scholar distinguished for delicate taste and epigrammatic felicity. In the altered stanzas the endings, with the exception of *make* for *take*, are the same as in Conington's; but this would weigh very little with me against retaining it: the chromatic effect of the quatrain as it stands—due to the mixture in more than usual abundance of the *oo* with the other open vowel sounds—is a better reason for its retention.

XXIV.] *Gemiscus*, like every other adjective (in this Ode, at least, I believe, without exception, unless (which is by no means certain) *horridi* in the 6th stanza constitutes one, is used, not otiosely as an embellishment, but *dramatically* or *dynamically*, to advance the action, so to say, and with special reference to the matter in hand, and is therefore properly translated so as to indicate that he has *both* his lamps (his own and his brother's) lit up, a condition precedent for the augury being favorable to the mariner. *Twin-lit*, *unshape*, and *whirls-in-one* are, I imagine, additions, and faultless ones, to our current speech, and destined, I venture to believe, to take rank with *invariant*, *covariant*, *contravariant*, and (word of wonder-working, cabalistic power!) *syzygetic*, and their train of followers, which have been struck at the same mint, and have met with universal recognition and acceptance. I may as well call attention to the strong prevalence of the *t* syzygy throughout the original poem, and its undesigned reproduction in the translation, and to the intenseness and concentration of thought and expression which can set in motion such a mass of ideas and feelings with the aid of no more than 305 Latin words, and even fewer if only detached sounds be reckoned as distinct words.

C

THE foregoing version is built upon the ruins of one made some twenty years ago, of which only 5 lines (57-61)—the porch of the old building—are retained in the present rendering. It is in the same metre as the late deeply regretted Prof. Conington's, which, having gone through three editions, and received the unstinted praise of English scholars and reviewers, I may have less scruple in criticising, as it cannot fail to find defenders—to my cost if I am wrong, and perhaps still more so if I am right. What I particularly object to in my predecessor's version as an entire departure from the spirit of his author, and the essence of lyrical poetry, is the continual substitution of the abstract for the concrete, the general for the particular, the oblique for the direct. 'Mæcenas mine!' addressed by a poet who knew his relative social position to his patron, in 3; the omission of any equivalent for *beatae* in XI., for *incertos* in LI., and for *Africis* in LVII.; 'reverberate to the enormous shock,' in 39; 'cancel' for 'diffinget' in 47; 'caresses' for 'honores,' and 'fickle dame' in 51 (an interpolation not even original, being given by Scriven, 1843),[*] are examples which could be easily extended of liberties which I should never have presumed to take

---

[*] So compare Conington's
    'And laughs should man's anxiety
      Transcend the bounds of man's short sight,
with Scriven's
    . 'And smiles when mortal's anxious tear
      Betrays too much a mortal's fear.'
Such coincidences can hardly be accidental. Professor Conington, who in his preface mentions Mr. Theodore Martin's version with high praise, never once alludes to Scriven's, which, though unquestionably inferior to the other as verse, is in many respects superior to it as a translation. There appears to be a common consent

with an author whom I respected sufficiently to translate, but may pass as comparatively minor blemishes. But how can any excuse be offered for such renderings as 'luxury' for 'divitibus,' in 13, 'Heaven' for 'Deus,' in 29, 'a river seaward borne' for 'fluminis delabentis Etruscum in mare' (stanza 9), 'stirred to madness' for 'irritat,' line 41, 'the morn may see' (l. 41), 'storms around my vessel rave,' for 'mugiat Africis malus procellis,' 57-58; anything less Horatian than such substitutions and inversions it is in my judgment impossible to imagine.

I believe the only way to obtain a tolerable translation of the English public-schoolboy's own book, which Horace is (just as much as Euclid unfortunately is or was in another direction), would be to parcel the work out among the members of a society who should each devote the labour of a year to effect the adequate rendering of a few hundred lines at most—the results to be submitted to the criticism and correction of the joint body to be periodically convened for the purpose.*

Another English scholar of deservedly high reputa-

---

among the English translators of Horace to ignore Mr. Scriven in their prefaces. This gentleman probably omitted to enrol himself as a member of any of the influential Societies of Mutual Admiration and Assurance (Unlimited) which undertake to guide the taste of the town.

* The number of existing translations and paraphrases may be reckoned by scores. Had each translator confined himself to a tithe of a single book of the Odes, the work might have been already accomplished. I regard the present accepted translations as doing positive mischief to the public, inasmuch as they tend to lower the standard of attainable correctness and degrade the ideal of translation. Think, too, of the gain to language by the resources to which a translator is driven who is obstinately bent on a faithful reproduction of his author.

tion has favoured the world with a rendering to which he gives the name of verse, but which being to my ears entirely without melody or rhythm, I should rather designate as harsh and distorted prose. Apparently unaware of the office of rhyme in marking off a line as a sort of compound foot (like a bar in music), and so aiding to sustain the measure, this gentleman refers to it patronisingly as 'an elegant ornament.' Only versifiers gifted with an ear peculiarly sensitive to time can afford to dispense with its aid: I remember reading a short poem of Mr. Matthew Arnold's 'On Growing Old,' half through, before I became aware, or could persuade myself previous to close examination, that the verse was unrhymed, an illusion consequent upon the consummate skill and accuracy with which the measure is sustained.

It does not seem to be at all understood among us in England—the land where, as I once heard Dr. Theodore Benfey observe, Genius abounds but Method takes no root—that versification has a technical side quite as well capable of being reduced to rules, as that of painting or any other fine art. In Miss Mitford's recently published correspondence, there is a letter in which she wonders at a 'travelling poetess' asking her for a book of rules on poetry. The wonder should rather have been at no such book (as far as I am aware) existing, or at all events being generally known to do so, in the English language, although we maintain a Professor of Poetry at one at least of our old Universities. There is quite as much room for the exposition of a method of distributing sound as of laying on colour, and indeed the analogy between the two arts of Versification and Coloring may be demonstrated to exist down to some very minute technical details. I may seek some other opportunity of stating the result of my speculations in this direction, and especially the principle of twofold — i.e. respiratory and sonorific—continuity in verse founded (as regards the less known law of *phonetic syzygy**) on the physical fact of the permanence† of the auditory impressions.

* The other law, which I call that of *anastomosis*, although little talked about, is no secret, being necessarily familiar to writers of words for song music and all judicious singing-masters, a great part of whose business it is to teach the art of keeping back the breath. Anastomosis gives to verse its cohesion, syzygy its flow and consistency. In a vague sort of way, we may call them the objective and subjective factors of verse harmony. Of course I am not unaware that there is a third source of phonetic beauty in verse (the highest of all), which depends on gradation of tones, on the agreeable succession of allied sounds (in especial, though not exclusively, vowel sounds), where the continuity is like that of the colours and tints in the solar spectrum, and the pleasure like that we feel in watching a sunset or seeing a peacock unfold its tail, or a rainbow glow and fade away in the sky. Some of the most beautiful and popular lines in Gray and Byron owe their chief charm to the prevalence of this element. *Metrik*, again, including the study of accents, pauses, and interruptions, may be referred to the antagonistic principle of discontinuity; and I need not add that continuity and discontinuity exercise parallel functions in the ideological province of versification to what they do in the purely technical department of the subject. There is also a third province of diction—expression and appropriateness, which lies between these two, just as in a ball-room dress, the shape and cut, the colours, ornaments, and flouncings, the texture and seams, all three form a separate province of study, corresponding to the ideology, the expression, and the texture of verse composition.

† This permanence, by the way, is the ground of the possibility of hypallage; transposed without it, consecutive sounds could not be shuffled back in the sensorium into their proper order of succession. Its existence, too, is proved directly by the bare fact of the sensuous pleasure (the so-called tickling of the ear) derived from rhyme. Alliteration and rhyme, it need scarcely be observed, are under one point of view only

46 Principles of Versification exemplified.

As regards metre, let us denote a spondee, the first epitrite, a dactyl, and a trochee, by A, B, C, D respec- extreme cases, or as we say in algebra, limiting forms of phonetic syzygy. It is, however, I consider, more correct to refer each of them to Symptosis, or the theory of clashes and beats. Anastomosis, Syzygy, and Symptosis are the three subdivisions of Synectic, as Synectic, Chromatic, and Metric are of Rhythm. So, too, Symptosis trifurcates into the theories of Beats or Jars, Assonances, and Rhyme; and again, Rhythm, Expression, and Idealistic (corresponding to Sound, Word, and Thought) are the three main divisions of Poetry as a whole. Without phonetic syzygy, rhythmical composition is no more like verse than shoddy is like cloth: it is this which gives the fibre and texture to versification, and explains the success of generally-accepted quotations, proverbial sayings, and happy repartees. Sounds must be regularly introduced and carried out of the verse-canvas: suspended, prepared, recalled, played with, as it were, before finally let go, concentrated, diffused, crossed, perplexed, and interlaced. It is of importance chiefly as a canon to the composer; but those who have to recite in public will find no small advantage to follow from a previous study of the syzygies, with a view, by subtle management of the voice and the introduction of almost imperceptible stresses on particular sounds, to give the fullest effect to the ruling harmonies of the verse. All real poets consciously or unconsciously give us sounds of 'linked sweetness long drawn out;' but we have some versifiers—and highly cried up, betitled, and decorated ones too—of the present day, who have no notion, explicit or implicit, of the law of syzygy, whose verses are accordingly utterly flabby and limp, as void of backbone as a jelly-fish, and fail to make any continuous or solid impression on the mind or organs of the hearer. The effect on the senses of the double continuity (conjunctive and objective, disjunctive and subjective), when well maintained and duly brought out, is something quite *sui generis* —a sort of transcendental substance—so intense in its action (if I may judge from my own sensations and the reported ones of the only fellow-versifier I have the advantage of knowing intimately) as to be capable of giving a spasm to the whole nervous system, like a lump of solidified carbonic acid gas placed on the palm of the hand, or the charge of an electrical machine passed through the arms and shoulders. Anastomosis gives a sort of rectilinear fibre to the web of verse in one direction, syzygy

Mathematical Harmony of Alcaic Stanza. 47

tively: then the construction of the Alcaic stanza, *as commonly practised by Horace* (allowing for the liberty of the final syllable of a line to be made long, which is only stealing from the natural interval of breath between two consecutive lines), will be represented by the scheme (or as, say, in determinants, the square matrix)—

$$\begin{matrix} A & B & C & C \\ A & B & C & C \\ A & B & D & D \\ C & C & D & D \end{matrix}$$

which (as is apparent) has a pure algebraical or tactical deep-seated harmony of its own. Denoting the lines of currilinear threads of connexion (or say lines of force) in the transverse direction. I have spoken above of beats and jars, —the former term (for which perhaps *congruence* would be a useful substitute) may be used to denote the relation of two sounds which forcibly recall each other in a legitimate or agreeable, the latter in an illegitimate or disagreeable connexion, *clash* being reserved as the generic term to include the other two. The source of the illegitimacy which exists seems to lie in a tendency to misdirect the ear by breaking up the rhythm. Thus, ex. gr., like sounds occurring in the 4th place of two tolerably contiguous lines, or in the 4th and 8th of the same or neighbouring lines, are in general objectionable in octosyllabic metre. Two like sounds in adjoining places, or when one of the couple is in the first place, rarely produce a jar. I believe it will turn out that the complete discussion of the theory of beats and jars depends on a refined doctrine of numerical ratios, the quantities which form the terms of the ratios being the quantities of time into which the line or lines in which the clashing elements occur, is or are divided by those elements reckoned as appertaining to the anterior portion of each such line. As a general rule it may be stated that the nearer the homologous quantities are to a ratio of equality without being actually equal, the better (just as in music a fifth is a better interval than a twelfth), and when the ratio is given, the smaller the common measure of the terms the better. The case of equal ratios belongs to a special theory. Also, it is obvious that on a distinct ground very strongly congruent elements must not lie too close to one another.

symbols by single letters, and reading the square upwards, the scheme assumes the type L M N N, which is homœomorphic with the upper two lines of the square. And again, using α, β, γ to denote the duads AB, CC, DD respectively, and counting only as one the repeated uppermost horizontal line, we obtain the complete combination system—

$$\alpha\beta$$
$$\alpha\gamma$$
$$\beta\gamma$$

Compare this remark with notes to XXXVI. and LXIV. as evidence of the strong mathematical bias of Horace's mind, wherein perhaps is to be sought the secret of the peculiar incisive power and diamond-like glitter of his verse. Had Athens been Cambridge, and Orbilius Colenso (whose private pupil at the University I was long before the far-famed Zulu was heard of), I have little doubt that Horace might have come out the Numa Hartog or Pendlebury of his year.

The annexed trifling translations from the German, or most of them, were done about the same time as the first and superseded form of the Horace-translation which precedes. I have not cared to incur the trouble and loss of time necessary to recast them according to my present more severe notions of a translator's duty of fidelity to his original.

Of the three first pieces, 'The Ideals' is, I believe, the most fairly open to censure on this ground. The last stanza of this, if I remember right, was an afterthought, and did not appear in Schiller's original edition of the poem—it seems to me only appended as sonorous ballast, to give greater weight and solemnity to the close, and I do not hold myself responsible, as a translator, for its emptiness or little worth of meaning. I heard with inexpressible rapt emotion, but yesterday, the manly colloquy between Wallenstein and Max (the Temptation scene), at the Harrow Speeches, and could hardly believe I was listening to the imitated accents of the author of the mawkish personification of Endeavour in 'The Ideals.' Schiller and Dryden, let me add Byron—who shall read your earlier and your later works, and say that a Poet is born and not made? We all know, too, the story of Alfieri's self-culture. All the world over, Art beats Nature.

II. THE IDEALS.—*Schiller.*

Ah ! wilt thou faithless from me sever !
  Ah ! wilt thou thus inexorably,
With all thy fancies fade for ever,
  With all thy pains and pleasures, fly ?*

* For a precedent (not known to me when I ventured upon 'inexorably') for the use of a final assonant tribrach, cf. Byron's 'Hebrew Melodies':—

> 'But we must wander *witheringly*,
>   In other lands to die,
> And where our fathers' ashes *be*
>   Our own may never lie.'

Any one happening to object to 'thus inexorably' may substitute for it 'with averted eye.' The terminal sound in *witheringly* or *inexorably* accords with the terminal sound *i* (in *it*) of the diphthong *i* (in *fie*), but not with what ought to be the pure vowel in *me*, which only by a vice of pronunciation not uncommon in

Nor yet a little linger near me,
  Oh! thou my youth's fresh aureate prime,
In vain! the waves still onward bear thee,
  On to the boundless Sea of Time!

Quenched now the suns serenely glowing,
  Whose light, life's orient path illumed;
And quelled th' inebriate heart, o'erflowing
  Whilst yet its loved Ideals bloomed!
For ever fled, once prized so holy,
  The faith in that, my spirit dreamed,
By the rude Real turned to folly,
  What once so fair, so heavenly seemed!

England can drawl itself out to resemble the vowel sound in 'it.' I am told by a great scholar (a principal ornament of Owen's College in Manchester) that *been* in rapid colloquy in the phrase 'I have been,' for example, almost invariably becomes *bin*. Honest Italian singing-masters find it especially difficult to make their English pupils maintain the purity of the vowel sounds. The greater number of them give it up in despair from the outset. Fashionable drawing-room Italian must be fun indeed to the exquisite Italian ear, but the Italians are a grave people and know how to keep their countenance, which they must do if they would keep their pupils. To return to the 'assonance' of 'inexorably' with 'fly'—why is it so faint, so infinitesimal? For a reason depending on a theory which, as far as I know, I have been the first to enunciate, viz. that the common definition of a diphthong, 'a complexion or *coupling of vowels* when the two letters send forth a joint sound, so as in one syllable both sounds be heard' (Ben Jonson), is quite defective, if not absolutely erroneous. Between a coupling of sounds and a diphthongal sound the interval is as wide as between a mechanical mixture and a chemical combination. The two marks of sound which connote a diphthong *are neither of them sounded*: they do but indicate the two *limits* from one of which to the

As when, enamoured of his creature
  Pygmalion hugged his statue bride,
Till through each pallid marble feature
  Sensation poured its glowing tide;
So I, in fond delirium often
  Wooed nature with a lover's zest,
Till she to warm, to breathe, to soften,
  Relented on this poet-breast;

And all its fervid transports meeting
  She who was dumb, an utterance found,
Gave back my lips' ecstatic greeting,
  And felt my heart's impassioned sound.
Then lived each tree, each flower flashed feeling,
  With silver fall, each fountain sang;
E'en soulless things, sensation stealing,
  With echoes of my spirit rang.

other the voice passes continuously in uttering the diphthong; it is the filling-up of the interval so symbolised which constitutes the diphthongal sound; and accordingly it is not every two vowel symbols which can be conjoined to represent a diphthong, but only such two as admit of a continuous uninterrupted passage of the breath from one limit to the other. A diphthong is a sound of an essentially different nature from a vowel or any combination of vowels. However rapidly two vowels are made to succeed each other, they will remain two vowels still, and never blend into a diphthong. The nearest analogue to the diphthong is the slur in vocal music. In general (I do not say always), a diphthong cannot be reversed as such; i.e. in the act of reversal it becomes a vowel syllable; but this is not surprising, seeing that we are equally unable to reverse the two initial sounds of a word like *praise*; if we attempt to do so, the word becomes a *dissyllable* (*repays*).

Then strove with might unseen, unseeing,
    A shapening world, this breast's confine,
To burst the bands that bound its being
    In word and deed, in sound and sign.
A shape, of what enchantment moulded,
    While with closed bud, its head reclined,
But ah! whose blossom now unfolded,
    Flaunts weak and withered in the wind.

Upsprang, by his bold spirit speeded,
    Blest in the madness of his dream,
By care unbridled, unimpeded,
    The youth o'er life's ecstatic scene;
Up to the faintest blue of heaven,
    To circling orbs that pale on high,
On wings of dauntless venture driven,
    He cleaves free passage through the sky.

How joyous then life's path appearing,
    As gaily he o'erleaps each bound,
While near his chariot wheels careering,
    Hope's airy escort dance around;
Love with the sweet reward entrancing,
    Fortune with gold crown dearly won,
Fame with her starry brow proud glancing,
    And Truth irradiant as the sun.

But ere midway the goal discerning,
    My treacherous guides began to stray,
And on their viewless steps returning,
    Stole softly one by one away:
Away, light-footed Fortune hurried;
    Unslaked my thirst at Wisdom's tide,
In doubts and clouds of error buried,
    Truth waned, then vanished from my side.

I saw profaned Fame's ensigns cover—
 Her halo gild—the Vulgar head;
And ah! too soon its springtime over,
 Love's hours of soft enchantment fled.
Then stiller wore and stiller ever,
 More steep and lonely still the way,
And fainter now the last gleams quiver
 Of Hope's declining, dying ray.

Of all who early thronged to guide me,
 Who in my hour of need stood fast,
Who hangs consoling still beside me,
 And follows to the grave at last?
'Tis thou! who healing aid still bearest,
 Friendship! who bindest up each wound,
Who lovingly life's burthen sharest,
 Thou, whom I earliest sought and found!

Thou, too, who passion's storms allayest,
 With Friendship freely mated ever,
Who laborest on, nor e'er destroyest,
 Busy, unwearied, stern Endeavour!
Who tho' but grains of sand thou heapest
 To swell the eternal pile sublime,
Yet from the mouldering record sweepest,
 Hours, days, and years of mortal time.

III. THE GOLDSMITH'S DAUGHTER.—*Uhland.*

A GOLDSMITH in his workshop stands
 Where pearl and ruby shine,
'The brightest jewel in my hands
 Thyself art still, Helena,
 Thou darling daughter mine!'

Steps in a knight of bravest mien—
'Good even, maiden fair!
And Master goldsmith too, good e'en !—
    A jewelled wreath, I prithee,
    Shape for my maiden's hair.'

And when the goldsmith's work was done,
    And sparkled bright the charm,
Helena soon as she's alone,
    With heaving bosom claspeth
    The wreath around her arm.

'Ah! wondrous happy lot is thine,
    Who shall this chaplet wear;
Ah! what delight, what joy were mine,
    Gave he me but a chaplet
    Of roses, I might wear.'

Not long before the knight came back,
    Approved the wreath and cried,
'I would, Sir goldsmith! ye would make
    A wedding-ring with diamonds
    For my enchanting bride.'

And when the wedding-ring was made,
    Glittering with diamond-stone,
She drew it sad and half afraid
    Upon her bridal finger,
    Soon as she was alone.

'Ah! wondrous happy lot is thine
    Who shall this token wear;
Ah! what delight, what joy were mine,
    Gave he me but a ringlet
    Of his own golden hair.'

Nor longer now the knight delayed
　　Well pleased the jewels eyed,
'Right fine, Sir goldsmith, ye have made
　　These precious true-love offerings
　　　For my enchanting bride.

'Beseech ye! beauteous maid, come near,
　　Think thou art she I woo,
On thee I'll test the bridal gear,
　　If well it may beseem her,
　　　For she is fair like you.'

On that same morn the maiden fair,
　　To grace the Sabbath day,
Was decked with more than wonted care,
　　As she to church was wending,
　　　Donned in her best array.

She blushing like a rose fresh blown,
　　Before the knight doth stand;
He sets on her the jewelled crown,
　　The ring upon her finger,
　　　Then takes her by the hand.

'Helena sweet, Helena dear,
　　The jest right out is played,
'Tis thou the wedding wreath shalt wear,
　　And thus I ring thy finger,
　　　My chosen, cherished maid!

'Here gold and pearl and precious stone
　　Have long encharmed thine eyes,
And well these tokens have foreshown
　　That ye with me to honour
　　　Shall higher yet arise.'

IV. CASSANDRA.—*Schiller*.

Joy ran high in halls of Ilion
   Ere the haughty fortress fell;
Song from all th' exulting million
   Shook the tuneful golden shell;
Wearying labor laid aside is,*
   Rests each hand from tearful strife,
Whilst the hero-souled Pelides
   Priam's daughter woos to wife.

---

* It is worthy of notice how by 'alliteration's artful aid' a construction which would otherwise offend the ear as forced is made to appear perfectly natural. Whoever has had any practice in versification knows that sounds exercise a perceptible attraction upon one another in the mind, or, so to say, a strong sound seeks to procreate another like unto itself: thus *labor* appears to demand *laid* to be brought into apposition with it, and the displacement of the copula passes unnoticed. Alliteration and the tendency of crimes to repeat themselves both alike belong to the wide category of *habit*, of which Newton's first law of motion exhibits the physical image. Why the *p* sound in particular tends to reproduce itself is a subject worthy of serious consideration. It is probably a purely physiological effect owing to the strength of the impression made on the sensorium during the suspension of breathing which the production of this sound demands. I have been told by my friend the eminent painter and academician, Mr. Solomon Hart, of a passage which he thinks he has met with in the 'Decline and Fall,' where the *p* begins a word no less than ten or eleven times in uninterrupted succession, and we have all read in Dickens of the Mrs. General who recommended Little Dorrit, in order to give a good form to her lips, to say sometimes to herself, before entering a room, 'papa, potatoes, poultry, prunes and prism, prunes and prism,' and to ignore the existence of anything that is not 'perfectly proper, placid and pleasant.'

Bearing laurel boughs they follow
  To the temples, throng on throng,
To the shrine of bright Apollo,
  To Thymbræus, God of song;
Through each alley echoes waking,
  Sounds of joy Bacchantic roll,
Whilst her moan unheeded making
  Sorrows on one mournful soul.

Joyless midst the joy prevailing
  The despised Cassandra roves,
Stung with sorrow unavailing,
  To Apollo's laurel groves;
In the forest's deep recesses
  Bursts into prophetic sound,
And the fillet from her tresses
  Casts indignant on the ground.

The second half of the stanza originally ran thus:—

> *Weary every hand abideth,*
> *Passing from the tearful strife,*
> *Whilst the hero-souled Pelides*
> *Priam's daughter woos to wife.*

I consider the imperfect rhyme of the first and third line in the above comparatively unimportant, inasmuch as the rhyming of the odd lines having only occurred once previously, the habit of expecting it has not had time to form in the sensorium of the hearer. Moreover, the sense of dissonance is almost effaced amidst the glare of the broad diphthongal consonance of the penultimate syllables. The metrical office of rhyme, i.e. the marking off of a bar of time, is sufficiently fulfilled, and any slight sensuous disappointment to the ear of an imperfect craving for accordance (like a duly resolved discord in music) is more than made up for by its complete gratification in the sequel.

'Mirth each fleeting terror chases,
　　Every heart beats high in cheer,
Hope relumes those timeworn faces
　　Sumptuous swells the bridal gear;
Me, alone of all the million
　　Me, no fond illusion waits,
For I see on swooping pinion
　　Ruin hover o'er their gates.

'I behold a torch-light glowing,
　　But not borne in Hymen's hand,
Flashes o'er the welkin throwing
　　All unlike to offering brand;
Banquets gaily they are spreading,
　　But in my prophetic mind
I can hear the Godhead treading,
　　Who shall hurl them to the wind.

'Sunk in speechless grief I languish,
　　Or to desert wilds repair,
For they chide my mortal anguish,
　　And they mock at my despair.
By the fortunate abandoned,
　　By the joyful held to scorn,
Thou too cruelly hast wantoned
　　Pythian! I too much have borne.

'Oh! Thou God relentless-minded,
　　Why unseal my spirit's sight
Midst a people ever blinded
　　With all senses barred to light.

Why impart the gift of seeing
  What no power may turn aside,
The foreshadowed must have being,
  The predestined must betide!

' 'Tis profane the cere-cloth riving
  Where a spectre lurks beneath.
Error is the law of living,
  Knowledge but a name for death;
Take, oh take thy mournful splendor,
  From mine eyes, the lurid gleam,
Cursed the mortal thou wouldst render
  Mirror to thy heaven-lit beam!

' Give me back my vision bounded,
  And my senses' duskened sheen
Song nor voice of joy I've sounded
  Since thy mouth-piece I have been;*
Thou the future hast imparted,
  But the present turned to pain,
Rifled me of youth light-hearted;
  Take thy treacherous gifts again!

' With the Bride's adornment never
  I my dewy locks might twine,
Since thy Priestess vowed for ever,
  I have served thy mournful shrine;

---

* Some friendly critic regards the phrase '*thy mouthpiece*' as an inadequate rendering of *deine Stimme*, or as a solecism in language; but I think it a fair approximation to the sense, and permissible in form, in the same way as we may speak of Miss Harriet Martineau being in England the mouthpiece of Comte, or Professor Huxley (besides the much more besides that he is in himself) a mouthpiece of the myriad-minded Darwin.

Grief my budding spring-time blighted,
    Youth exhaled in sighs unblessed;
Every pang that near me lighted
    Thrilled from my responsive breast.

'Sportive joy of soul revealing,
    All around me live and love
In the youthful tide of feeling;
    Me, but pain and sorrow move,
Nor for me the spring reviving
    Spreads o'er earth its festive green;
Who that owns to joy in living
    Down its dark abyss has seen!

'Happy in her blind delirium,
    In her hopes ecstatic blessed,
To enclasp the dread of Ilium
    As a bridegroom to her breast;
See my sister's heart proud swelling,
    Vainly struggling calm to seem;
Scarce yon Gods, there o'er us dwelling,
    Hails she happier in her dream!

'I've too gazed on him entreating
    Whom my yearning heart desired,
And have shared the blissful greeting
    By the glow of love inspired.
But to nuptial dwelling never
    With the loved one might depart,
For a Stygian shadow ever
    Cast its baleful gloom athwart.

'Spectres gaunt and shapes ungainly
   Flock from Tartarus' shores to me,
Seeking rest or roaming vainly
   From the grisly bands to flee;
Through the youthful sports and babble,
   Still the phantom troop would steal;
Shuddering grim and hideous rabble,
   Howe'er could I joyous feel!

'I behold the death-steel glitter,
   And the murderer's visage glare,
Can ne'er flitting hither, thither,
   'Scape that portent of despair,
Nor my rooted gaze unfasten:
   Fixed, foreboded, fearless scanned,
To fulfil my doom I hasten,
   Falling on the foemen's land.'

Whilst her plaintive tones thus wander,
   Hark! what deafening shouts arise!
At Apollo's portal yonder,
   Stretched a corpse, Achilles lies.
Discord's gory crest proud towers,
   The protecting Gods are gone,
Thunder breaks and darkness lowers
   O'er devoted Ilion.

V. COMFORT IN TEARS.—*Goethe.*

Whence comes it, thou thus pensive art
    While all else glad appears?
Too well we see, in those sad eyes
    The tell-tale trace of tears.

'And tho' I lonely may have wept,
    Mine only is the smart;
The tears that trickle down so sweet,
    Relieve my gushing heart.'

Thy joyous friends beseech thee come,
    Oh! come unto our breast;
There safe, whatever loss has happed,
    Unburthen thy unrest.

'Your mirthful fancies ill divine
    What makes my bitter pain;
Ah! no, 'tis not what I have lost,
    But what I cannot gain.'

Wake then, and call thy courage up,
    Time hath not dulled thy soul;
With thy fresh life, man has the strength
    And will, to win the goal.

'Ah! no, the goal I cannot win,
    It looms too distant far;
It dwells so high, it shines so bright
    As yonder dazzling star.'

Miscellaneous Examples. 63

The stars one should not covet them,
 But glory in their light;
And with enraptured gaze look out
 Into the cloudless night.

' And with enraptured gaze I look,
 So many a garish day;
For weeping, leave me still the night,
 So long as weep I may.'*

HAVING since the preceding matter was in type stumbled upon the original free (I should now say, over-free) rendering of *Tyrrhena regum*, together with a similar one of a portion of *Impios parrae* (Hor. iii. 27), done at about the same period, and certain other similar effusions, I may as well take this opportunity of ridding my hands of this lumber of unconsidered trifles, which, after all, reviewing them as impartially as I (the author of their being) am able to do, seem to me not vastly inferior in sense and expression to many of the vamped-up, far-fetched, transcendental inanities of some of the third-class poetasters of the day which find a ready echo in the press. If Joseph Scaliger thought himself qualified in his twice-edited ' Cyclometrica Elementa ' to attempt the Quadrature of the Circle, said to have been ' victoriously refuted by Vieta,' by way of teaching their business to the geometricians of his time, and

---

* As it seems to be a womanish sort of youth (possibly, even a girl in boy's clothes) who is speaking, I have allowed more so's to stand than might otherwise have been justifiable. It ought to be expressly laid down in future editions of ' Mary's Grammar' that *so* is the feminine transcendental pluperfect form of superlative, as, ex. gr. *lovely, lovelier, loveliest, so lovely,* or *such a love.*

Thomas Hobbes, though with a better intention, laid himself open, on a like ground, to refutation and censure, I may hope to be excused crossing over, from the other side,* the border-line between scholarship and science, and for submitting, with a less ambitious aim and in a much more humble frame of mind, some of my long-forgotten (*d'outre-tombe*) transgressions in verse and rhythmical speculations to the inspection of my hoped-for private-circle century of indulgent readers.†

As I shall most probably never take up pen again on the subject of Verse, I may as well embrace this opportunity of making a brief profession of faith concerning modern Metric and what are termed accentual feet. I am satisfied, then, that on this subject Edgar Poe is perfectly right in the principles laid down by him in his 'Rationale of Versification,'‡ that the substratum

* Chronology, leading straight to Astronomy, I presume was Vieta's crossing-point: Synectic, which leads down from the Alps of Cauchy and Riemann to the flowery plains of Milton and Byron, my own.

† When the above was set up in print it was my intention only to publish 100 copies for private distribution, and I might have persisted in this intention had I not felt that the remarks I have passed on the labours of others rendered it imperative upon me to face the consequences of the public avowal of my opinions.

‡ He ought to have called it 'Rationale of Metre.' Rhythm, used in its most general sense to signify the purely technical part, one of the three main heads of versification, itself subdivides again into three branches—synectic, chromatic, and metric, the latter including accent, quantity, and suspension; which last again subdivides into the theories of rests, stops, and pauses. Metric guards the ear, Synectic satisfies, Chromatic charms it. The first ensures correctness, the second organization, the last beauty and embellishment. For the benefit of my non-mathematical readers, I may state that 'Synectique' is a word used,

of measure is time; that an accented syllable is a long syllable, and that an unaccented syllable is a short one of varying degrees of duration, and that feet in modern metre are of equal length. Professor Newman is of an opposite opinion, and goes the length of saying, that *accent* is so far from lengthening that it even tends to *shorten* syllables, instancing the first syllable in female' as shortened by the accent, and of course implying that it is shorter in fémale than it would be in femále: to argue against such an assertion (which I think no one who is not time-deaf will be found to concur with) would be like reasoning upon colours with one who is born colour-blind.*

and I believe for the first time, by Cauchy in his Theory of Functions, the true and very insufficiently acknowledged foundation and origin of Riemann's great doctrine of Continuity, in like manner as the Triads of Kant appear to me to contain the germ (impossible to have escaped ulterior development) of the method of Hegel; or, as I am told, Turner had not existed but for Claude. At the opposite pole to Rhythm, as previously observed, we have the Idealistic of Verse, which has its continuity and discontinuity branches (the analogues of Synectic and Metric, to attempt to go into any analysis of which here would lead me too far), intermediate to which lies Imagery, the analogue of Chromatic. Ex. gr. Construction, Deduction, Development, Action, and Invention, will belong to the continuity branch; Distribution, Transition, Contrast, Light and Shade, Quantification, &c. to the discontinuity one. Between Rhythm and Idealistic, as also already noticed, lies Expression (sense clothed in sound). At the base of and giving nourishment to our poetical plant, lies Emotion, at once the root and crown of lyric verse.

* If it be true, as Professor Newman alleges, 'that an English voice cannot dwell on accented syllables without seeming to drawl,' it must be because of the *difficulty* of getting over the accented syllable in right time, in consequence of the tendency to be *over* delayed by giving effect to the accent.

But in reckoning the length of feet, attention must be paid to the time expended in preparing and closing, as well as in actually emitting the sound, and also to the silent syllables or pauses, to which Poe has not paid sufficient attention. I believe that his theory of substitution is perfectly correct; that, to use musical nomenclature (which appears not to have been familiar to him), an iambus with us is a quaver and crotchet; a trochee, a crotchet and quaver; an anapaest, so called (when substitutable for an iambus, of which many examples will be found in my preceding Horatian version);* two semi-

---

* It may be noticed that all the anapaests therein employed are convertible, by elision or contraction, into iambic feet. A pretty copious sprinkling of such equivocal anapaests (as I am used to call them) helps to confer lightness and dignity on octosyllabic metre, much in the same way as raised heels are said to be worn by the young ladies of the period, to give spring and distinction to their gait, *and to add to their height*. I have noticed that in the two first letters in the 'Essay on Man,' Pope in no single instance, as far as I can recollect, allows contraction to take place by elision or by two contiguous vowels in a word running into one another; every word is made to contain its maximum number of syllables. Pope, I imagine, would have rejected as *incorrect* such a line as

'Have linked that amorous power to thy soft lay,'
and as downright *false*,

'While the jolly Hours lead in propitious May.'

The Rev. Mark Pattison has kindly informed me that in Pope's Satire I., in 156 lines there are 24 commencing with -◡, and only two cases of accent or weak syllable in any other position. I remember reading, when a child, in some common English school-book, that a trochee in iambic verse was only permitted at the beginning of a line. (By the way, why is it that we cannot conversely substitute an initial iamb for a trochee, in a trochaic line?) I have recently been told by a high authority,

Metre reduced into Terms of Music. 67

quavers followed by a crotchet, and a dactyl, substituted for a trochee, a crotchet followed by two semiquavers. Poe even quotes cases (very unsatisfactory ones, in my opinion, borrowed from unknown American versifiers), where a quaver is resolved into a triplet. Such cases, however, do exist, as ex. gr. in the imaginary line, 'And earth the o'erpowering tones rehearse;' in [ering] each syllable is a semiquaver, but in [the o'er] only the third of a quaver. I think also, that there are some lines which occur, chiefly in very modern poetry, where the principle of *apocopation* must be applied to the scanning, and others, where that of *tempo rubato* is intended or necessary to give full effect to the recital.

The principle of the *silent* syllable, or to speak more intelligibly, of the *rest*, removes all the anomalies or supposed imperfections of metre which Edgar Poe imagined to exist (and they are purely imaginary) in the opening lines to the 'Bride of Abydos.'* He has

that a trochee is admissible anywhere in an English iambic line, subject to the sole condition that two trochees shall not occur in succession. I believe the safer rule to be that in general a trochee should only occur at the beginning of a line, or after a pause or close of a period, or when the second part of the foot is a monosyllable or ends a word, the ground of the exception in all these cases being the same, and involving the theory of the *rest*.

* ' Know ye the land where the cypress and myrtle
    Are emblems of deeds that are done in their clime,
  Where the rage of the vulture, the love of the turtle,
    Now melt into sorrow, now madden to crime?
  Know ye the land of the cedar and vine,
  Where the flowers ever blossom, the beams ever shine;
  Where the light wings of Zephyr, oppressed with perfume,
  Wax faint o'er the gardens of Gul in her bloom;
  Where the citron and olive are fairest of fruit,
  And the voice of the nightingale never is mute;

made the exceedingly interesting observation, that all these lines run into one another, and so read will be found to consist of a succession of accentual dactyls. He rightly understands (collected works, vol. ii., p. 242), that *crime* at the end of the fourth line, and *tell* at the end of all, are to be understood as what he calls ' cæsuras;' in plain English, each takes on two quaver rests. ' fume, Wax ' in the seventh and eighth lines, he rightly regards as a spondee substituted for a dactyl, or, as I should say, two crotchets for a crotchet and two semi-quavers.

But he makes a difficulty, for which there is no occasion, about the words 'twine, And,' (ll. 14, 15) which he says 'is false in point of melody,' for that ' we must force " And " into a length which it will not naturally bear.' The fact is, that *twine* ending a line, very naturally takes after it a *quaver rest*, a slight pause which assists the effect, by enabling the reciter to take a short breath, so that what Poe supposes to be a spondee is virtually a dactyl. A similar remark applies to the words ' sky, In ' belonging to a triad of lines, which for some unexplained reason are dropped by Poe, and also to the words ' done? Oh ! ' which he scans as a spondee, but which is really a dactyl, ' Oh ! ' being a quaver preceded by a quaver rest. So in the seventh line of

> Where the tints of the earth, and the hues of the sky,
> In colour though varied, in beauty may vie,
> And the purple of Ocean is deepest in dye;
> Where the virgins are soft as the roses they twine,
> And all, save the spirit of Man, is divine?
> 'Tis the clime of the East, 'tis the land of the Sun—
> Can he smile on such deeds as his children have done?
> Oh! wild as the accents of lovers' farewell
> Are the hearts which they bear and the tales which they tell.'

'Paradise Lost,' 'of Oreb, or of Sinai, didst inspire,' I consider that *eb* and *or* are both quavers, and that the *comma* between them represents a quaver rest. So, again, I consider that the most eligible scanning upon Poëan principles of the admired line 56 in my version of *Tyrrhena regum*, 'Poverty portionless but pure,'—is crotchet, two semiquavers; quaver-rest, crotchet; two semi-quavers, quaver, quaver-rest; quaver, crotchet; as shown in the subjoined arithmetical scheme:—

$$1 \; \tfrac{1}{4} \; \tfrac{1}{4} \; | \; (\tfrac{1}{2}) \; 1 \; | \; \tfrac{1}{4} \; \tfrac{1}{4} \; \tfrac{1}{2} \; (\tfrac{1}{2}) \; | \; \tfrac{1}{2} \; 1$$

Thus much for my general notions about Metric, except that I ought to add, that as by force of association imaginary rhymes (such as *far* and *war*, *brood* and *flood*) pass muster even to the ear, so there are cases of imaginary time, where the measure is rather imputed than computed, and number usurps the function of, or in a Mahaffo-Kantian* sense may be said to schematise, duration.†

I may be pardoned for adding, in conclusion, that the

---

* I allude here to the sense ascribed to Kant's use of the word 'schematism' by the learned and accomplished Professor Mahaffy in his most truly valuable introduction to Kuno Fischer's Commentary on Kant. Kant is like a rainbow—every man sees his own. Had Kant studied versification, as (if I remember right) Socrates did in his youth, he would have learned the art of using words. No philosopher or savant need blush to give some time to the practice of this art, if he sets any value upon the faculty of rendering himself intelligible to the bulk of mankind.

† I think, too, that (as a rule) the ear, by an almost unconscious act of cerebration, attends to and takes note concurrently of *number* and *time*, accent and quantity, combined in metre. If we lay stress on either of these elements too exclusively, our theories will be sure to err.

experiment which called these renderings and observations into present being, turned out eminently successful, and that the recital of the Ode before an audience of several hundred men and women, boys and girls, with few exceptions belonging to the labouring classes, was received with great applause, thereby demonstrating *à posteriori* the justness of the musical principles upon which the version was constructed. This recital formed only one ingredient out of an extensive and varied bill of fare, consisting of songs, glees, performances on the pianoforte, rehearsals from Shakespeare and modern authors, in prose and verse, etc.* Of all the performances that took place, it was universally admitted that next to 'That Rogue Riley,' a comic song sung by a gifted young lady, Horace's 'Invitation to Maecenas to pass a Day with him in the Country,' called forth the greatest demonstration of public favour, and as I was told by some military friends who were present from the neighbouring garrison, the very National School children in the front rows, who

* I think the excellent and humanising influence of Penny Readings would admit of an easy and important development by being turned into Penny Gatherings. Besides recitations, works of art might be exhibited, and new songs or pieces of music, and poems or other forms of literary composition, submitted to a preliminary essay, and principles of criticism be introduced and discussed. How useful this would be, alike to authors and their audience! I remember dipping not long ago, for want of anything better to do, into the oration 'Pro Archia,' from which it seems that it was the custom in antient times for eminent orators or poets to give free recitations of their works to the people of the towns through which they passed. My proposed Penny Gatherings (where tea and coffee also might be made to circulate at a trifling expense) would serve a somewhat similar purpose.

poked their fun over Marc Anthony's Funeral Oration on Julius Caesar, were too much awed to laugh, and looked on and listened in rapt and solemn wonderment. The meaning of the proper names had been previously explained to them, and the situation brought home to their understandings by aid of a modern parallel. Thomas Moore did duty provisionally for Horace, and the Marquis of Lansdowne, Lord President of the Council, for Maecenas.

VI. INVITATION TO MAECENAS.—*Horace.**

Tyrrhenian progeny of kings,
    Wine mellowed with a jealous care
Roses and what choice essence flings
    Odors of Araby o'er the hair;

Wait thee Maecenas—why delay?
    Must Tibur, Aesula's steep plain,
And heights of Telegon alway
    Thee, from our Sabine farm detain?

Leave sumptuous pomp and the proud pile
    That seeks to mount into the skies;
Leave Rome its smoke and din awhile
    With village scenes to cheer thine eyes.

---

* This looser translation, thrown off at a white heat, cost me probably about as many minutes only as the preceding exact one half-hours or hours, and yet an uncritical eye will probably see little difference between the two. It is the last turn of the screw, and the blow of the hammer which is to drive the nail home, that call for the only real exertion of strength.

72 *Principles of Versification exemplified.*

> The rich love change—less dainty fare
> And walls undraped with purple woof,
> Oft smoothe the wrinkled brow of care
> Under the plain thatched peasant's roof.
>
> Now Cepheus shows his light again,
> Now Procyon blazes in the south,
> The Lion shakes his frantic mane
> And summer fields lie parched with drouth.
>
> The weary shepherd seeks the shade,
> Leads to the brook and thickets dank
> His languid flock, nor winds invade
> But all lies hushed upon the bank.*
>
> Thou, what with public weal accords
> And Rome's defence provid'st from far,
> Lest Seric or wild Bactrian hordes
> Or Tanaïs roll the tide of war.

---

* Poor cheery old Silvanus has got left out in the cold here. It was the remonstrance (not unaccompanied with encouragement) against this unjustifiable omission by a most learned and accomplished professor (crowned with recent laureate honors by an illustrious foreign Academy) at our most antient University, to whom I showed these lines, that awakened in me the dormant sense of a higher ideal of fidelity in translation. Just about the same time, too, the newspapers of the day were full of an account of an altar to the worthy old god, which had been found in the bed of the river Wear, in the North of England, which made his exclusion (when every other proper name received its due share of notice) the more invidious. 'Twas like being left out by an old friend from a dinner-party, to which all your mutual acquaintance have been invited.

O'er all, the future may impart
    Wise Gods have clouds and darkness thrown,
And smile when feeble mortals start
    At shadows of the dim unknown.

Live to the present—all besides
    Is drifted like the changeful wave
That now in smoke mid-channel glides
    Seeking Etruscan shores to lave.

Now with uprooted tree and stone,
    Cattle and houses swept from shore
Into an eddying torrent grown
    Shakes woods and rocks with maddening roar.

Lord of himself and blest shall prove
    He who can boast 'I've lived to-day
'To-morrow let dispensing Jove
    Cast o'er the skies what tint he may

'Sunshine or cloud! the work begun
    And ended may his power defy,
He cannot change nor make undone
    What once swift Time has hurried by.

'Fortune whose joy in mischief lies,
    Grown hardened in her cruel game
Changes from hand to hand the prize
    Smiling on each in turns the same.

'Welcome to stay! but if she shake
    Her fickle plumes—wrapped in my pride
I scorn her gifts and spotless make
    Unportioned poverty my bride.

'Not mine, when towering topmasts roar
   'Neath Afric's storms with piteous prayers
Or bargaining vows each God to implore
   Lest Cyprus' or fine Tyrian wares

'Add treasure to the ravening seas.
   Me shall my bounding pair-oared craft
With favouring Pollux and the breeze
   Safe through the tossed Aegaean waft.'

VII. TO SPRING.—*Schiller*.

Welcome beauteous youth
Nature's darling child!
Welcome on the verdant plain
With thy wealth of wood-flowers wild!

Here meeting thee again
My heart with joy runs o'er
For thou art come again
And smiling as of yore.

Know'st thou the maiden still?
Ah! canst thou friend forget?
'Twas here she loved me well,
That maiden loves me yet.

To deck my maiden's brow
Choice flowers I asked of thee;
I come and ask again
And thou! thou giv'st them me.

Then welcome beauteous youth !
Nature's darling child;
Welcome on the verdant plain
With thy wealth of wood-flowers wild!

THE annexed translation was worked out between a young Moravian clergyman who tenanted a contiguous attic to my own in the city of New York and myself.

My friend, who was at work for the newspaper called the *New York World* appealed to me from time to time for a word or a rhyme as a poet is apt to do from any bystander, when he has clenched his fists, knit his brows and despairingly thrown up his eyes to the ceiling in search of inspiration, which will not come, all in vain. It ended in my getting warmed and interested in my friend's work and after taking taking the pen out of his hand pretty well dashing off in hot haste the translation given below, whereby I was made conscious for the first time of the possession of a traductory power of the existence of which within me I was until then entirely unconscious, as much so as the innocent Faublas of a productive faculty of quite another kind, before his first lesson after the evening of the ball.

VIII. TO THE DANUBE.—*Blumauer*.

OH ! joy, that I, thou German stream !
May hail thee, kinsman true,
Who doubts thy kin to our dear land,
Come and thy image view.

Come view the German pride of soul
　　Thou in thy bosom bearest,
When like the German heart aroused
　　Thy angry waves thou rearest.

The German giant-march behold
　　In thy majestic course,
And point what race more kin to thee
　　E'er started from its source:

Or see thee eager to the deep
　　Thy seven fond arms expand,
And say who more resemble thee
　　In friendship's sacred band.

Then viewing how beneath the wave
　　Thy modest bosom swells,
Exclaim, within thy veiled career
　　Germania's spirit dwells.

Joy! then that I thou ancient flood
　　May still thy praise renew,
And still in thee my race invoke
　　Its imaged self to view.

IX. THE HOSTESS' DAUGHTER.—*Uhland*.

THREE friends who were students crossed over the Rhine
To the house of a hostess where they went in:

' Bring out Mother Hostess! good cyder and wine
But where is that beautiful daughter of thine?'

'My cyder and wine run sparkling and clear,
But my daughter lies there, stretched out on her bier.'

And when they went in to the fair maiden's room,
Lo! she lay dead and dressed for the tomb.

The first student drew her veil on one side
And wistfully gazing the dead maiden eyed,

'Oh! wert thou but living thou beautiful maid
Henceforth how dearly I'd love thee,' he said.

The second one covered her face up again,
And turned round and wept, in piteous strain:

'I loved thee so fondly, this many a year,
And alas! thou now liest stretched on thy bier.'

The third one once more, her veil drew aside,
Then kissed her pale cheek, and passionate cried,

'I loved thee long fondly, I love thee yet still,
And love thee for ever and ever I will.'

X. THE DEATH-LOCK.—*Rückert.*

'Eh' ihr sie ins Grab müsst sinken,
 Gebet mir die Locke nur!'

Ere the earth close o'er thee,
 Maiden loved and fair!
Leave me, I implore thee,
 This one lock of hair.

Thou, lock! so lately thrown
  In shadow round her brow,
Its glory shed and flown
  Thine, how lustrous now!

Nought else of her but will
  To the tomb repair;
But thou! unfaded still
  Freely float in air.

Frail as thou appearest,
  Tress so finely wove,
Thou the burthen bearest
  Of a heaven of love!

One lingering last caress
  Let my fondness share,
Then, wind thou sacred tress
  Round this ring I wear.

Turning this magic toy
  She whom I adore,
Radiant with love and joy,
  Springs to sight once more.*

---

* I have taken considerable liberty with the number and time elements of the metre in the above, but I do not find the result offend my ear. For the intermixture of iambic and trochaic lines (although upon a more exact plan) a friend reminds me that there is Horatian precedent, as also familiar examples in Milton and Ben Jonson. The version is rather a paraphrase than a translation.

I BELIEVE in the earlier stanzas of the annexed version there are some patent errors of interpretation. I remember being told so at the time when it was composed, at which period I was even less conversant with German than at present, and had no dictionary at hand, but only my inward consciousness, to appeal to. We have not Uhland at the Athenæum Club, and I do not possess a copy of my own to enable me to correct my errors. So I let the piece pass forth as it originally came out of my hands. I cannot read it without some emotion myself, and therefore presume that it must possess a certain synthetic fidelity of tone and feeling, albeit defective in verbal conformity to, or even correct perception in some passages, of the meaning of the original. The third stanza always brings back to my mind St. Mary's at Cambridge, as I used to see it, when an undergraduate, by moonlight.

XI. THE CASTLE BY THE SHORE.[*]—*Uhland.*

Hast thou the castle beholden
　The castle by the shore,
Where roseate hues and golden
　Over the turrets soar;

Beetling as though it might fall
　Into the mirror-bright stream
Or rise like a giant tall
　And melt in the evening beam.

[*] Mr. Longfellow, I am informed, has translated this poem, but to the best of my recollection I have not seen his translation.

Oh! yes, the castle I've seen
    Lifting its spectral head,
When above the moon hath been
    And around dim clouds were spread.

Beating against the sea-wall,
    Made the winds music gay?
Sounded from the castle-hall
    The lute and festive lay?

The winds and the waves hushed all,
    Like an infant asleep were lying,
But a sigh from the castle-hall
    Came blent with a piteous sighing.

Saw'st thou the bride with the king,
    A joyous measure tread,
The sheen of the golden ring
    And their mantles dyed with red?

Welcomed they not with delight,
    Nuptials of one so fair,
More beauteous than morning light,
    Streaming with golden hair?

The father and mother I saw,
    Their garments with black were dyed,
The crowns from their heads withdraw,
    But never saw more the bride.

Anonymous Poems. 81

THE annexed and subsequent trifling pieces marked *Anonymous* come from obscure sources as, long ago, a roving fancy may have dictated, and it would not be worth while to affect to ascertain and *afficher* the original authorship of rhymes here reproduced, as a better sort of nonsense-verses, for the sake of exemplifying syzygetic principles. In the Acrostic following the piece below any practised ear will at once notice the prevalence of a ruling N sound, the character imparted by which is a certain mildness and serenity, as in the T sound we may detect a sort of vitreous quality of strength. The compound key N T, as we may call it, is one of frequent occurrence, and forms a peculiarly natural and agreeable combination. Cf. the opening stanzas of the version of Europa, the last piece of the collection. I imagine it would not be difficult, on examination, to ascertain the favorite syzygetic key of any of our more finished poets.

XII. THE EVENING STAR.—*Anon.*

WHY ask me, fair and gentle maid,
   Friend to my soul and song!
Who chief in elegance arrayed
   Adorned the festive throng?

When Venus seated in the sky
   Amidst the starry choir,
Turns on the rapt uplifted eye
   Her gracious orb of fire,

And looks from out night's vaulted brow
   A queen above the rest,
How canst thou fail untaught to know
   The loveliest, brightest, best?

XIII. ACROSTIC.—*Anon.*

Joy! happy mother, that indulgent Heaven
Unto thy love, so dear a child hath given.
Serenely bright, like yon pure starry way
That shines with lustre lovelier than the day;
Innocent joy be still her treasured dower,
Nor ever evil, staining that sweet flower,
Alloy the golden gleam of life's fair opening hour!

XIV. WINTER.—*Anon.*

When winter treads his dreary round
   And cold congeals the air
And snows lie deep upon the ground
   And woods wave bleak and bare,

When winds in angry warfare meet
   And clouds obscure the sun
And pining for their vital heat
   The streams forget to run,

Say! were it best my constant friend
   Of heart unfeigned, and pure!
Cowering beneath the blast to bend
   Or manfully endure:

And still through winter's dreariest gloom
   A cheerful trust maintain
That Heaven will smile, the woodlands bloom
   And spring come round again.

XV. TO AN INK-SPOT UPON A LADY'S CHEEK.

Anon.

Where tender-hued emotion's tide
  Mirrors the soul within,
Why seek, dull spot! the bloom to hide
  Or veil the lustrous skin?

Why on that rose with envious spite
  Pillow thy ebon head,
Shadowing the soft and sunny light,
  Those orbs of feeling shed?

Pencilled with clouds, the azure vault
  But beams more heavenly pure,
And spots upon the sun exalt
  The brightness they obscure.

Presumptuous spot! some elsewhere seek
  A meaner flower to stain,
Nor hope to mar this matchless cheek
  Where youth and beauty reign.

Here dwells a secret sacred charm,
  All ill intents to foil;
No touch of malice, here can harm
  No spot of envy soil.

XVI. MELANCHOLY.—*Anon.*

Oh, why my fair and only love
  Thus heaves thy gentle breast?
That tender bosom where the dove
  Of peace should build her nest.

Like one whom inward thoughts oppress
  Thou smotherest oft a sigh,
And at the name of happiness
  A tear starts to thine eye.

As if there lay within the word
  Some secret power to wound,
You shudder like a startled bird
  Whene'er I breathe the sound.

No more the joyous sunbeams dance
  In those once playful eyes;
They flame—but with a fitful glance
  Lighting Hope's obsequies.

Upon thy uncomplaining brow
  Sits melancholy throned,
And every feature tells of woe
  Those lips have never owned.

Some nourished pain thou shunn'st to speak
  Shadows thy rising years,
And spreads a paleness o'er thy cheek
  More pitiful than tears.

So young, so lovely, and caressed
  Whence can thy sorrow spring,
What scorpion touch of grief has pressed
  To those soft veins its sting?

Oh! but to feel thy heart beat sound
  Washed clear from every stain,
My lips would suck the venomed wound
  And all its poison drain;

The mortal anguish I'd endure
  And triumph 'midst my pain,
Could I but so thy sorrows cure
  And see thee smile again!

XVII APRIL 30.—*Anon.*

Once more the breath of spring
  With fragrance fills the air,
And birds on happy wing
  Trill forth their paeans clear.

The swelling buds disclose
  Their treasures garnered long,
The balmy west wind blows
  The trembling boughs among.

And gaily through the mist
  The cheerful sun doth break,
Like lover who has kissed
  The tears off beauty's cheek.

In vain for me the while
  The rustling zephyrs play,
Or opening blossoms smile
  To welcome back the May:

In vain the sun doth slant
  Down the green sward his beam,
And the winged choir descant
  Their gaily carolled theme.

Banished from looks which fell
   Like dews from heaven on me,
And lips whose tones could swell
   My soul to ecstasy,

The pomp of vernal skies
   Is powerless to win
This heart where feeling dies
   And winter dwells within.

XVIII. INDIFFERENCE.—*Anon.*

Or give me praise or give me blame
   Each I would learn to bear,
But teach me not that hateful name
   Indifference to hear.

Indifference wars against the plan
   Decreed by powers above,
When God in love created man
   And bade him live by love.

Spread o'er the earth its soft attire
   With song inspired the groves
Lent to the orbs of eve their fire,
   And blessed each thing that moves.

By no indifferent hand designed,
   Such joys to man were given,
But from a free and bounteous mind,
   Spontaneous grace of Heaven.

His love was with thee at thy birth
    And formed thee what thou art;
His love still walks with thee on earth
    And glows within thy heart;

Sheds on thy cheek its varying hue
    Soft lustre on thine eye;
Smiles on those lips more soft to view
    Than sunset in the sky;

Bids Nature teach thee skill to know
    The beautiful and true,
And Art her magic mantle throw
    On all within thy view.

When Chaos was, ere yet the light
    Had dawned upon the day,
Indifference sat o'er cloud and night
    In solitary sway.

But when Night fled as one ashamed,
    And Chaos' rule was o'er,
The voice of Heaven itself proclaimed
    Indifference rules no more.

Then give me praise or give me blame
    Each I will learn to bear,
But force me not that hateful name
    Indifference to bear.

XIX. REMONSTRANCE.—*Anon.*

Oh! why those narrow rules extol?
    These but restrain from ill,
True virtue lies in strength of soul
    And energy of will.

To all that's great and high aspires,
  Prompts to the path of fame
From Heaven draws down Promethean fires
  And wraps the soul in flame.

With brow erect, eye undismayed
  Confronts the midday sun,
Nor sleeps inglorious in the shade
  Of praises cheaply won;

Scans not too curiously the chance
  Of good or evil fate,
But with a free and fearless glance
  Knocks at Hope's golden gate;

The truthful course pursues and knows
  By Heaven-imparted light,
And scorns to shape to outward shows
  Its conscious sense of right.

Still, while it renders Reason's name
  The meed of honour due
Forgets not sacred instincts claim
  Their share of reverence too.

The frown of unjust censure braves,
  Retreats not with the tide,
But nobly stems and stills the waves
  Of prejudice and pride.

XX. FAITH.—*Anon.*

Nor earth, nor air, nor seas, nor fire,
  Nor aught that fate can interpose
  Nor open scorn nor secret foes
Shall tear me from my heart's desire.

Like those antique imperial dyes
   Which age nor use can e'er efface,
   But win from Time a nobler grace,
Stamped on my soul, thy image lies.

While Faith still vivifies this frame,
   Or Memory prompts one soul-felt sigh
   And Hope looks upward to the sky,
This heart shall beat, for thee the same.

No mortal strength nor skill can sever
   The link which kindred atoms binds,
   Nor less, congenial kindred minds,
United once, are one for ever.

XXI. KEPLER'S APOSTROPHE.—*Anon*.

Yes! on the annals of my race,
   In characters of flame,
Which time shall dim not nor deface,
   I'll stamp my deathless name.

The fire which on my vitals preys,
   And inly smouldering lies,
Shall flash out to a meteor's blaze
   And stream along the skies.

Chafed as the angry ocean's swell
   My soul within me boils,
Like a chained monarch in his cell,
   Or lion in the toils.

To wealth, to pride, to lofty state,
    No more I'll bend the knee,
But Fortune's minions, meanly great,
    Shall stoop their necks to me.

The God which formed me for command,
    And gave me strength to rise,
Shall plant His sceptre in my hand,
    His lightning in my eyes;

Shall with the thorny crown of fame
    My aching temples bind,
And hail me by a mighty name
    A monarch of the mind.

Me, heaven's bright galaxy shall greet
    Theirs by primordial choice,
And earth the eternal tones repeat
    Of my prophetic voice.

Stung in her turn, the heartless fair
    Who proudly eyes me now,
Shall weep to see some other share
    The godhead of my brow;

Shall weep to see some lovelier star
    Snatched to my soul's embrace,
Ascend with me Fame's fiery car
    And claim celestial place.

Tune oh! my soul thy loftiest strain,
    Exult in song and glee,
For scorn has snapped each earthlier chain
    And set the immortal free.

Minds destined to a glorious shape
  Must first affliction feel;
Wine oozes from the trodden grape,
  Iron's blistered into steel;

So gushes from affection bruised
  Ambition's purple tide,
And steadfast faith unkindly used
  Hardens to stubborn pride.

XXII. FROM THE ITALIAN.

Occhi! stelle immortali,
Cagione de' miei mali!
So chiusi m' ammazate,
Aperti che fareto!

Eyes, like stars in heaven that glow,
Eyes, creators of my woe!
If e'en closed, my soul ye slew,
What, wide open, would ye do!

XXIII. WHAT'S IN A NAME?—*Anon*.

In names a mystic virtue lies
Concealed but clear to loving eyes,
And sounds have influence to control
The inmost workings of the soul.

The voice which breathes thy name in air,
Speaks thou art gentle, good, and fair,
Mild as the fragrant breeze in May,
Or earliest blushes of the day.

The guardian angel at thy birth,
When first he welcomed thee on earth
Rapt in the wonder of thine eyes
Murmured a Ha! of pleased surprise.

But grieved that one like angels fair
The mortal soil of earth must share,
And e'en thy star of beauty set
Sighed out an ah! of fond regret.

Attendant spirits hovering nigh
Caught up the murmur and the sigh,
With two dull links the sounds brought near
And stamped the name, each loves to hear.

Whichever way we turn that name
It speaks to eye and soul the same;
It tells of honesty and truth,
Unaltering innocence of youth.

XXIV. THE STORY OF EUROPA.*

Hor. Od. III. xxvii. 25.

Snow-white midst Ocean's monster-brood,
　Set sidelong on the crafty steer,
At mantling perils of the flood,
　The bold Europa paled with fear.

She who but now culled meadow-flowers, [5
　And for the Nymphs, vowed garlands wove,
Sees nought in twilight's dusky hours,
　Save billows round and stars above!

So when to mighty Crete she came, [9
　The hundred-citied, 'Father!' cries,
'Oh! forfeit filial tie and name,'
　Whilst fury flashes from her eyes.

---

* I quote the subjoined argument from honest old Lemprière:—'Europa, a daughter of Agenor, King of Phoenicia and Telephassa. She was so beautiful that Jupiter became enamoured of her, and the better to engage her affections, he assumed the shape of a bull, and mingled with the herds of Agenor, while Europa and her female attendants were gathering flowers in the meadows. Europa caressed the beautiful animal, and at last had the courage to mount upon his back. The god took advantage of her situation, and retiring towards the shore, crossed the sea, with Europa on his back, and arrived safe in Crete. Here he assumed his original shape, and declared his love. The nymph, a stranger on an unknown shore, consented (although she had once made vows of perpetual celibacy), and became the mother of Minos, Sarpedon, and Rhadamanthus.' Could anything be more regular and satisfactory?

'Whence come and where? One death were gain [13
    Lost maiden honour to redeem;
Weep I awake, a suffered stain,
    Or mocks me guiltless, a vain dream,

'Flit through the *ivory* porch of sleep? [17
    Which were the happier choice to prove,
To crop the freshly flowering heap,
    Or o'er long wastes of sea to rove?

'Oh! that the monster near me stood, [21
    Too fondly loved now loathed again!
This steel I'd crimson with his blood,
    And rend his milk-white horns in twain.

'Shameless I fled my father's home, [25
    Shameless 'scape death—oh! hear my prayer,
And grant, some God! that I may roam
    Naked where lions make their lair;

'Ere from my form the juices drain, [29
    Or foul decay my fair cheeks soil,
Let tigers hunt me o'er the plain,
    But beauteous still, devour their spoil.'

Cries, 'vile Europa! Why delay?' [33
    My far-off Sire—'on yon ash nigh
In virgin zone, well fetched away,
    Go wrench thy neck and pendent die:

'Or trusting to the whirlwind's breath, [37
    If rocks and reefs more charm thy soul,
Fall on these ledges lined with death;
    Else, take the shame of carding wool,

'Handmaid to some barbarian dame,   [41
   And harlot of a royal line;'
With loosened bow, young Love now came,
   And Venus with a laugh malign.

Who, when enough she had mocked the fair: [45
   Said 'Hush thy wrath, no more complain;
The hateful bull, since such thy prayer,
   Yields thee his horns to rend in twain:

'Of mighty and all-conquering Jove   [49
   Know thou art consort, sobs forswear;
Learn worthy thy proud state to prove,
   Earth's fractioned orb, thy names shall bear.'

NOTES.

2. *Medias fraudes.*] Very difficult to interpret, for there are four different meanings attributed to *medias*, viz. 'intervening,' 'enveloping,' 'midway,' 'laid open;' and three to *fraudes*, viz. 'frauds,' 'damages,' 'dangers;' making twelve combinations in all to choose from. The commentators at my command give no help (as I find is usual with them in any case of real difficulty); and Forcellini fails me. Some people tell me that *medias* means *peripheral*—that the frauds in the middle of Europa, or Europa in the middle of the frauds, is, by poetical licence, all one. I once thought *medias* must mean 'intermediate,' in the sense of referring to the frauds which intervened between her playing with the bull and her finding herself where she was; but then, I asked myself, was she in a position to turn pale at thoughts of anything that had happened? were not all her thoughts and emotions concentrated on the present? Professor Key tells me that the old meaning of *fraus* is 'damage,' and that the word is employed here in that sense. I should have thought this was rebutted, by *doloso* preceding; but I bow to so great an authority, which also is supported by Newman's 'midway mischiefs,' and to some extent

also by Professor Conington's, who, as not unusual with him, goes off, not at a tangent, but at an asymptote, and gives as the equivalent for *medias fraudes*, 'the yawning grave.' What if the old Delphin version of *apertas* for *medias*, and Scriven's *fraudes displayed* (the very heart of the fraud, as one might say, 'the very heart of the machine'), were the true conception, after all? Yielding (although entirely unvisited by a single ray of conviction from 'the illative sense') to my *à priori* faith in the correct judgment, in such a matter, of Key, Newman, and Conington, i. e. accepting their interpretation of *fraudes*, I take *fraudes medias* to mean *dangers ahead, perils on her path*—midway between where she is and (not where she was, but) wherever she may unconsciously be drifting to. I can understand how *medias* X's may come to mean *surrounding* X's, in the manner following: If an X is intermediate between me and anywhere I may be going to, then (like the case of differentiating a function, *à la* Cauchy, all round a point) I am enveloped by X's, and so *medias fraudes* may come to mean *enveloping 'fraudes,'* a medium, a net-work of 'fraudes,' 'fraudes' encompassing me all round about.

14.] *Virginum culpa* I understand to refer to loss of character consequent upon Europa being thrown an unprotected female on an island with its hundred cities swarming with the dangerous sex. I maintain fearlessly in opposition to the dark and unwarrantable imputations cast by Professor Newman on the conduct of the heroine, and still more on the taste of the elegant recounter of the story, that it contains no reference to any worse conduct on the part of Europa than, Clarissa-like, allowing herself to be thoughtlessly carried off from her father's house by the back door. The words 'Credidit tauro latus,' 'Nuper in pratis,' 'quae simul tetigit,' 'unde quo veni,' not unsupported also by the sneering words 'zonâ bene te secutâ,' give a complete account of her actions and establish an irrefragable *alibi* as regards the *locus in quo* for any improper purpose, from the time of her sidling on the bull's back to the moment of her being landed on shore, and momentarily abandoned by the instrument of her abduction, At the end of her burst of rage, after she has had a good cry, Jupiter reappears (in his own character) like a prince restored to his proper form and throwing off his disguise in the retransformation or *dénouement* scene of a pantomime, and Venus with her boy is the good fairy, all in white with crown on head and sceptre in hand, who smiles on the reunited lovers and assures and consecrates their mutual happiness. With the odious view Professor Newman has chosen to take of Horace's treatment of the subject, why did he trouble himself to introduce any part of it into his translation; why not have left it alone altogether?

Professor Newman in his preface vindicatory of his peculiar mode of translation says, ' some approximation may be attained which gives to the reader not only a knowledge of the substance but a feeling of the *form of thought* and a right conception of the *antient tone of mind*.' Has he favored the world with this torso of the beautiful original in order that the rising age might not lose the benefit of the form of thought and antique tone conveyed by his interpolated, ' heavenly Venus stood at her side, and soft words whispered of MYSTIC COMFORT, which dream not *thou* to hear'? What moral right had Mr. Newman to put such words into the mouth of his author, and to substitute his own pedantic mode of rivetting the story to its prooemium, the jewel to his setting, for the graceful and poetical *abandon* of his inimitable original? Was this just to Horace, or fair to his readers? It reminds one of the King of Portugal, who would have taught God a simpler and a better plan of constructing the Universe had he stood by and been consulted on the day of creation.

47.] '*Dolose ao maligno,*' *sed juncta ironia, non enim irata adveniet Venus,*' says the excellent Orelli *à propos* of ' perfidum ridens.' This then we see is the exact counterpart of the French *sourire malin*, and offers a good occasion of introducing the idiom into our own language.

52.] Why *nomina* in the plural? Once I thought it might be simply *idiomatic*, as we say ' style and title ;' again, I thought it was possibly poetical amplification, or magnification—a sort of reflected ascription of plurality—an attempt to stretch out a name, to make it fit to clothe so vast a subject as the *Orbs terræ*. Then, again, I thought it was possibly a logical consequence of the partibility of a name—of the fact that every syllable of a name is itself a name—a thing by which the bearer of the name may be known—' and airy tongues that syllable men's names.' Nay, I found some were of opinion that the plural was contrary to sense and introduced only for the sake of euphony and metre. But I think now that the true solution is neither idiomatical nor poetical nor logical, nor metrical, but transcendental—intended as a gratification of that sense of the manifold in unity (equally the delight of Mariolater and Methodist) which is the chief source of religious ecstasy, as the converse principle—that of unity in the manifold—is of philosophic exaltation. The phrase *rectus orbis* raises the conception of division—of a frontier line between Europe and the rest of the world. Wherever, on one side, along this frontier line, or within it, one might ask the general name of the place, 'Europa' we should hear in reply: a painted map would be starred all over with 'Europas'—as many 'Europas' as kingdoms or subdivisions of the Continent, the name swarming everywhere, like the Bourbon *fleur-de-lys* or the 'T. M.' of the Catholic sovereigns. The passages from Horace and Ovid quoted by Orelli, both referring to Icarus, corroborate this manner of interpretation, as each island in the sea belonging to him would, as it were separately, assert his name. This view justifies me, I think, in preserving the plural form of the word in the translation, and so getting a soft *s* into the line. The much-abused sibilants—the hard and soft *s* or *z* sounds—are for English verse what his glazes, or I believe I ought to say his varnish, are for the painter (is there not a sort of analogy between sibilance and glare, or tendency to crackle?): they are the indispensable menstruum for giving unity and continuity to the surface of the canvas; but of course care must be taken, in the one case as in the other, not to overvarnish.

56.} I join with Orelli and Macleane in applauding this honest burst of feminine feeling, the heroic and martyr-like regard to the conservation of her good looks, which is a woman's first duty to her sex, and to her prerogative of upholding in herself and others the type of physical perfection, which in the long run brings moral and intellectual perfection too, in its train. I well remember hearing the late agreeable and clever octogenarian Madame ———, a connection by marriage of the Bonaparte family (whom she strikingly resembled in feature), express herself to me with some disdain of her American countrywomen, who, as she said, marry a man 'because they like him and admire his good looks, whereas in Europe girls marry for rank and social position.' This lady, who had imbibed European notions, evidently thought it was rather a vulgar taste in women to admire beauty, strength, and stature in a man, or, at all events, to act on such a feeling. She was, in my opinion, quite wrong; and her countrywomen, in taking heed of their natural instincts in the matter, are performing a high moral duty, of which society reaps the benefit.

INAUGURAL PRESIDENTIAL ADDRESS

TO THE

MATHEMATICAL AND PHYSICAL SECTION

OF THE

BRITISH ASSOCIATION AT EXETER,

August, 1869.

INAUGURAL PRESIDENTIAL ADDRESS,

&c. &c.

LADIES AND GENTLEMEN,—

A few days ago I noticed in a shop window the photograph of a Royal mother and child, which seemed to me a very beautiful group; on scanning it more closely, I discovered that the faces were ordinary, or, at all events, not much above the average, and that the charm arose entirely from the natural action and expression of the mother stooping over and kissing her child which she held in her lap; and I remarked to myself that the homeliest features would become beautiful when lit up by the rays of the soul—like the sun 'gilding pale streams with heavenly alchemy.' By analogy, the thought struck me that if a man would speak naturally and as he felt on any subject of his predilection, he might hope to awaken a sympathetic interest in the minds of his hearers; and, in corroboration of this I remembered witnessing how the writer of a well-known article in the 'Quarterly Review' so magnetised his audience at the Royal Institution by his evident enthusiasm that, when the lecture was over and the applause had subsided, some ladies came up to me and implored me to tell them what they should do to get up the Talmud; for that was what the lecture had been about.

Now, as I believe that even Mathematics are not much more repugnant than the Talmud to the common apprehension of mankind, and I really love my subject, I shall not quite despair of rousing and retaining your attention for a short time if I proceed to read (as, for greater assurance against breaking down, I shall beg your permission to do) from the pages I hold in my hand.

It is not without a feeling of surprise and trepidation at my own temerity that I find myself in the position of one about to address this numerous and distinguished assembly. When informed that the Council of the British Association had it in contemplation to recommend me to the General Committee to fill the office of President to the Mathematical and Physical Section, the intimation was accompanied with the tranquillizing assurance that it would rest with myself to deliver or withhold an address as I might think fit, and that I should be only following in the footsteps of many of the most distinguished of my predecessors were I to resolve on the latter course.

Until the last few days I had made up my mind to avail myself of this option, by proceeding at once to the business before us without troubling you to listen to any address, swayed thereto partly by a consciousness of the very limited extent of my oratorical powers, partly by a disinclination, in the midst of various pressing private and official occupations, to undertake a kind of work new to one more used to thinking than to speaking (to making mathematics than to talking about them), and partly and more especially by a feeling of my inadequacy to satisfy the expectations that would be raised in the minds of those who had enjoyed the privilege of hearing or reading the allocution (which fills me with admiration and dismay) of my gifted predecessor, Dr. Tyndall, a man in whom eloquence and philosophy seem to be inborn, whom Science and Poetry woo with an equal spell, and whose ideas have a faculty of arranging themselves in forms of order and beauty as spontaneously and unfailingly as those crystalline solutions from which, in a striking passage of his address, he drew so vivid and instructive an illustration.

From this lotos-eater's dream of fancied security and repose I was rudely awakened by receiving from the editor of an old-established journal in this city, a note containing a polite but peremptory request that I should, at my earliest convenience, favour him with a 'copy of the address I proposed to deliver at the forthcoming meeting.' To this invitation, my first impulse was to respond very much in the same way as did the 'Needy knife-grinder' of the 'Antijacobin,' when summoned to recount the story of his wrongs to his republican sympathiser—'Story, God bless you, I have none to tell, Sir!' 'Address, Mr. Editor, I have none to deliver.'

I have found, however, that increase of appetite still grows with what it feeds on, that those who were present at the opening of the Section last year, and enjoyed my friend Dr. Tyndall's melodious utterances, would consider themselves somewhat ill-treated if they were sent away quite empty on the present occasion, and that, failing an address, the members would feel very much like the guests at a wedding-breakfast where no one was willing or able to propose the health of the bride and bridegroom.

Yielding, therefore, to these considerations and to the advice of some officially connected with the Association, to whose opinions I feel bound to defer, and unwilling also to countenance by my example the too prevailing opinion that mathematical pursuits unfit a person for the discharge of the common duties of life and cut him off from the exercise of Man's highest prerogative, 'discourse of reason and faculty of speech divine,'—rather, I say than favour the notion that we Algebraists (who are wont to regard each other as the flower and salt of the earth) are a sot of mere calculating-machines endowed with organs of locomotion, or, at best, a sort of poor visionary dumb creatures only capable of communicating by signs and symbols with the outer world, I have resolved to take heart of grace and to say a few words, which I hope to render, if not interesting, at least intelligible, on a subject to which the larger part of my life has been devoted.

The President of the Association, Prof. Stokes, is so eminent alike as a mathematician and physicist, and so distinguished for accuracy and extent of erudition and research, that I felt assured I might safely assume he would, in his Address to the Association at large, take an exhaustive survey, and render a complete account, of the recent progress and present condition and prospects of Mathematical and Physical Science at home and abroad. This consideration narrowed very much and brought almost to a point the ground available for me to occupy in this Section; and as I cannot but be aware that it is as a cultivator of pure mathematics (the subject in which my own researches have chiefly, though by no means exclusively, lain*) that I have been placed in this Chair, I hope the Section will patiently bear with me in the observations I shall venture to make on the nature of that province of the human reason and its title to the esteem and veneration with which through countless ages it has been, and, so long as Man respects the intellectual part of his nature, must ever continue to be, regarded.†

It is said of a great party leader and orator in the

* My first printed paper was on Fresnel's Optical Theory, published in the *Philosophical Magazine*; my latest contribution to the *Philosophical Transactions* is a memoir on the 'Rotation of a Free Rigid Body.' There is an old adage, 'purus mathematicus, purus asinus.' On the other hand, I once heard the great Richard Owen say, when we were opposite neighbours in Lincoln's Inn Fields (doves nestling among hawks), that he would like to see *Homo mathematicus* constituted into a distinct subclass, thereby suggesting to my mind sensation, perception, reflection, abstraction, as the successive stages or phases of protoplasm on its way to being made perfect in Mathematicised Man. Would it sound too extravagant to speak of perception as a quintessence of sensation, language (i.e. communicable thought) of perception, mathematic of language? We should then have four terms differentiating from inorganic matter and from each other—the Vegetable, Animal, Rational, and Supersensual modes of existence.

† Mr. Spottiswoode favoured the Section, in his opening address, with a combined history of the progress of Mathematics and Physics; Dr. Tyndall's address was virtually on the limits of Physical Philosophy; the one here in print is an attempted faint adumbration of the nature of Mathematical Science in the abstract. What is wanting (like a fourth sphere resting on three others in contact) to build up the ideal pyramid is a discourse on the Relation of the two branches (Mathematics and Physics) to, their action and reaction upon, one another, a magnificent theme with which it is to be hoped some future President of Section A will crown the edifice, and make the tetralogy (symbolizable by $A + A', A', A, A.A'$) complete.

House of Lords that, when lately requested to make a speech at some religious or charitable (at all events a non-political) meeting, he declined to do so on the ground that he could not speak unless he saw an adversary before him—somebody to attack or reply to. In obedience to a somewhat similar combative instinct, I set to myself the task of considering certain recent utterances of a most distinguished member of this Association, one whom I no less respect for his honesty and public spirit than I admire for his genius and eloquence,* but from whose opinions on a subject which he has not studied I feel constrained to differ. Goethe has said—

'Verständige Leute kannst du irren sehn:
In Sachen, nämlich, die sie nicht verstehn.'

Understanding people you may see erring—in those things, to wit, which they do not understand.

I have no doubt that had my distinguished friend, the probable President-elect of the next Meeting of the Association, applied his uncommon powers of reasoning, induction, comparison, observation, and invention to the study of mathematical science, he would have become as great a mathematician as he is now a biologist; indeed he has given public evidence of his ability to grapple with the practical side of certain mathematical questions; but he has not made a study of mathematical science as such, and the eminence of his position and the weight justly attaching to his name render it only the more imperative that any assertions proceeding from such a quarter, which may

* Although no great lecture-goer, I have heard three lectures in my life which have left a lasting impression as master-pieces on my memory—Clifford on Mind, Huxley on Chalk, Dumas on Faraday.

appear to me erroneous, or so expressed as to be conducive to error, should not remain unchallenged or be passed over in silence.*

He says 'mathematical training is almost purely deductive. The mathematician starts with a few simple propositions, the proof of which is so obvious that they are called self-evident, and the rest of his work consists of subtle deductions from them. The teaching of languages, at any rate as ordinarily practised, is of the same general nature—authority and tradition furnish the data, and the mental operations are deductive.' It would seem from the above somewhat singularly juxtaposed paragraphs that, according to Prof. Huxley, the business of the mathematical student is from a limited number of propositions (bottled up and labelled ready for future use) to deduce any required result by a process of the same general nature as a student of language employs in declining and conjugating his nouns and verbs—that to make out a mathematical proposition and to construe or parse a sentence are equivalent or identical mental operations. Such an opinion scarcely seems to need serious refutation. The passage is taken from an article in 'Macmillan's Magazine' for June last, entitled 'Scientific Education—Notes of an After-dinner Speech,' and I cannot but think would have been couched in more guarded terms by my distinguished friend had his speech been made *before* dinner instead of *after*.

The notion that mathematical truth rests on the

* In his *éloge* of Daubenton, Cuvier remarks, 'Les savants jugent toujours comme le vulgaire les ouvrages qui ne sont pas de leur genre.'

narrow basis of a limited number of elementary propositions from which all others are to be derived by a process of logical inference and verbal deduction, has been stated still more strongly and explicitly by the same eminent writer in an article of even date with the preceding in the 'Fortnightly Review,' where we are told that 'Mathematics is that study which knows nothing of observation, nothing of experiment, nothing of induction, nothing of causation.' I think no statement could have been made more opposite to the undoubted facts of the case; that mathematical analysis is constantly invoking the aid of new principles, new ideas, and new methods, not capable of being defined by any form of words, but springing direct from the inherent powers and activity of the human mind, and from continually renewed introspection of that inner world of thought of which the phenomena are as varied and require as close attention to discern as those of the outer physical world (to which the inner one in each individual man may, I think, be conceived to stand in somewhat the same general relation of correspondence as a shadow to the object from which it is projected, or as the hollow palm of one hand to the closed fist which it grasps of the other), that it is unceasingly calling forth the faculties of observation and comparison, that one of its principal weapons is induction, that it has frequent recourse to experimental trial and verification, and that it affords a boundless scope for the exercise of the highest efforts of imagination and invention.*

* The annexed instance of Mathematical euristic is, I think, from its intrinsic interest, worthy of being put on record. The so-called canonical representation of a binary quartic of the

Lagrange, than whom no greater authority could be quoted, has expressed emphatically his belief in the importance to the mathematician of the faculty of

eighth degree I found to be a quartic multiplied by itself, together with a sum of powers of its linear factors, just as for the fourth degree it was known to be a quadric into itself, together with a sum of powers of its factors; but for a sextic a cubic multiplied into itself, with a tail of powers as before, was not found to answer. To find the true representation was like looking out into universal space for a planet desiderated according to Bode's or any other empirical law. I found my *desideratum* as follows: I invented a catena of morphological processes which, applied to a quadric or to a quartic, causes each to reproduce itself: I then considered the two quadrics and two quartics to be noumenally distinguishable (one as an automorphic derivative of the other) although phenomenally identical. The same catena of processes applied to the cubic gave no longer an identical but a distinct derivative, and the product of the two I regarded as the analogue of the before-mentioned square of the quadric or of the quartic. This product of a cubic by its derivative so obtained together with a sum of powers of linear factors of the original cubic, I found by actual trial to my great satisfaction satisfied the conditions of canonicity, and it was thus I was led up to the desired representation, which will be found reproduced in one of Prof. Cayley's memoirs on Quantics, and in Dr. Salmon's lectures on Modern Algebra. Here certainly induction, observation, invention, and experimental verification all played their part in contributing to the solution of the problem. I discovered and developed the whole theory of canonical binary forms for odd degrees, and, as far as yet made out, for even degrees too, at one evening sitting, with a decanter of port wine to sustain nature's flagging energies, in a back office in Lincoln's Inn Fields. The work was done, and well done, but at the usual cost of racking thought—a brain on fire, and feet feeling, or feelingless, as if plunged in an ice-pail. *That night we slept no more.* The canonisant of the quartic (its cubic covariant) was the first thing to offer itself in the inquiry. I had but to think the words 'Resultant of Quintic and its Canonisant,' and the octodeeadic skew invariant would have fallen spontaneously into observation;* Gauss has called mathematics a science of the eye, and in conformity with this view always paid the most punctilious attention to preserve his text free

my lap. By quite another mode of consideration, M. Hermite subsequently was led to the discovery of this, the key to the innermost sanctuary of invariants—so hard is it in Euristic to see what lies immediately before one's eyes. The disappointment weighed deeply, far too deeply, on my mind, and caused me to relinquish for long years a cherished field of meditation; but the whirligig of time brings about its revenges. Ten years later this same Canonisant gave me the upper hand of my honoured predecessor and guide, M. Hermite, in the inquiry (referred to at the end of this address) concerning the invariantive criteria of the constitution of a Quintic with regard to the real and imaginary. By its aid I discovered the essential character of the famous amphigenous surface of the ninth order, and its bicuspidal unicursal section of the fourth order (otherwise termed the bicorn), as may be seen in the third part of my Trilogy, printed in the *Philosophical Transactions*.

* I was under the conviction that a passage to that effect from Lagrange had been cited to me some years ago by M. Hermite of the Institute of France; on applying to him on the subject, I received the following reply:—

'Relativement à l'opinion que suivant vous j'aurais attribuée à Lagrange, je m'empresse de vous informer qu'il ne faut aucunement, à ma connaissance, l'en rendre responsable. Nous nous sommes entretenus du rôle de la *faculté d'observation dans les études que nous avons poursuivies de concert pendant bien des années*, et c'est alors, sans doute, que je vous aurai conté une anecdote que je tiens de M. Chevreul. M. Chevreul, allant à l'Institut dans la voiture de Lagrange, a été vivement frappé du sentiment de plaisir avec lequel ce grand géomètre lui faisait voir, dans un travail manuscrit, la beauté extérieure et artistique, si je peux dire, des nombreuses formules qui y figuraient. Ce sentiment nous l'avons tous éprouvé en faisant, avec sincérité, abstraction de l'idée analytique dont les formules sont l'expression écrite. Il y a là, n'est-il point vrai, un imperceptible lien qui rattache au monde de l'art le monde abstrait de l'algèbre et de l'analyse, et j'oserai même vous dire que je crois à des sym-

Dependence of mathematics on observation. 111

from typographical errors; the ever to be lamented Riemann has written a thesis to show that the basis of our conception of space is purely empirical, and our knowledge of its laws the result of observation, that other kinds of space might be conceived to exist subject to laws different from those which govern the actual space in which we are immersed, and that there is no evidence of these laws extending to the ultimate infinitesimal elements of which space is composed. Like his master Gauss, Riemann refuses to accept Kant's doctrine of space and time being forms of intuition,* and regards them as possessed of physical and

pathies réelles, qui vous font trouver un charme dans les notations d'un auteur et des répulsions qui éloignent d'un autre, par l'apparence seule des formules.'

I am, however, none the less persuaded that on one or more than one occasion, M. Hermite, speaking of Lagrange, expressed to me, if not as I supposed on Lagrange's, then certainly on his own high authority, 'that the faculty of observation was no less necessary for the successful cultivation of the pure mathematical than of the natural sciences.' I am glad also to notice that Lagrange was able to accommodate a friend *dans sa voiture*. England has much to learn from France and Russia as to the proper mode of treating its greatest men.

* It is very common, not to say universal, with English writers, even such authorised ones as Whewell, Lewes, or Herbert Spencer, to refer to Kant's doctrine as affirming space 'to be a form of thought,' or 'of the understanding.' This is putting into Kant's mouth (as pointed out to me by Dr. C. M. Ingleby), words which he would have been the first to disclaim, and is as inaccurate a form of expression as to speak of 'the plane of a sphere,' meaning its surface or a superficial layer, as not long ago I heard a famous naturalist do at a meeting of the Royal Society. Whoever wishes to gain a notion of Kant's leading doctrines in a succinct form, weighty with thought, and free from all impertinent comment, should study Schwegler's *Handbook of Philosophy*, translated by Stirling. He will find in the

objective reality. I may mention that Baron Sartorius von Waltershausen (a member of this Association) in his biography of Gauss ('Gauss zu Gedächtniss'), published shortly after his death, relates that this great man was used to say that he had laid aside several questions which he had treated analytically, and hoped

same book a most lucid account of Aristotle's doctrine of matter and form, showing how matter passes unceasingly upwards into form, and form downwards into matter; which will remind many of the readers of *Nature* of the chain of depolarisations and repolarisations which are supposed to explain the decomposition of water under galvanic action, eventuating in oxygen being thrown off at one pole and hydrogen at the other (it recalls also the high algebraical theories in which the same symbols play the part of operands to their antecedents and operators to their consequents): at one end of the Aristotelian chain comes out πρώτη ὕλη, at the other πρῶτον εἶδος. We have, then, only to accept and apply the familiar mathematical principle of the two ends of infinity being one and the same point (like the extremities of a divided and extended ring), and the otherwise immovable stumbling-block of duality is done away with, and the universe reintegrated in the wished-for unity. For this corollary, which to many will appear fanciful, neither Aristotle nor Schwegler is responsible. We perfectly understand how in perspective the latent polarities of any point in a closed curve (taken as the object) may be developed into and displayed in the form of a duad of *quasi* points or half-points at an infinite distance from each other in the picture. In like manner we conceive how *actuality* and *potentiality* which exist indistinguishably as one in the *absolute* may be projected into seemingly separate elements or moments on the plane of the human understanding. Whatever may be the merits of the theory in itself, this view seems to me to give it a completeness which its author could not have anticipated, and to accomplish what Aristotle attempted but avowedly failed to effect, viz. the complete subversion of the 'Platonic Duality,' and the reintegration of matter and mind into one.

to apply to them geometrical methods in a future state of existence, when his conceptions of space should have become amplified and extended; for as we can conceive beings (like infinitely attenuated bookworms* in an infinitely thin sheet of paper) which possess only the notion of space of two dimensions, so we may imagine beings capable of realising space of four or a greater number of dimensions.† Our Cayley, the

---

* I have read or been told (I believe erroneously) that eye of observer has never lighted on these depredators, living or dead. Nature has gifted me with eyes of exceptional microscopic power, and I can speak with some assurance of having repeatedly seen the creature wriggling on the learned page. On approaching it with breath or finger-nail it stiffens out into the semblance of a streak of dirt, and so eludes detection.

† It is well known to those who have gone into these views that the laws of motion accepted as a fact suffice to prove in a general way that the space we live in is a flat or level space (a 'homaloid'), our existence therein being assimilable to the life of the bookworm in a flat page; but what if the page should be undergoing a process of gradual bending into a curved form? Mr. W. K. Clifford has indulged in some remarkable speculations as to the possibility of our being able to infer, from certain unexplained phenomena of light and magnetism, the fact of our level space of three dimensions being in the act of undergoing in space of four dimensions (space as inconceivable to us as our space to the suppositious bookworm) a distortion analogous to the rumpling of the page. I know there are many, who, like my honoured and deeply lamented friend the late eminent Prof. Donkin, regard the alleged notion of generalised space as only a disguised form of algebraical formulisation; but the same might be said with equal truth of our notion of infinity in algebra, or of impossible lines, or lines making a zero angle in geometry, the utility of dealing with which as positive substantiated notions no one will be found to dispute. Dr. Salmon, in his extension of Chasles' theory of characteristics to surfaces, Mr. Clifford, in a question

central luminary, the Darwin of the English school
of mathematicians, started and elaborated at an early

of probability (published in the *Educational Times*), and myself
in my theory of partitions, and also in my paper on Barycentric
Projection in the *Philosophical Magazine*, have all felt and
given evidence of the practical utility of handling space of four
dimensions, as if it were conceivable space. Moreover, it should
be borne in mind that every perspective representation of figured
space of four dimensions is a figure in real space, and that the
properties of figures admit of being studied to a great extent, if
not completely, in their perspective representations. In philosophy, as in aesthetic, the highest knowledge comes by faith. I
know (from personal experience of the fact) that Mr. Linnell or
Madame Bodichon can distinguish purple tints in clouds where
my untutored eye and unpurged vision can perceive only confused
grey. If an Aristotle, or Descartes, or Kant, assures me that he
recognises God in the conscience, I accuse my own blindness if I
fail to see with him. If Gauss, Cayley, Riemann, Schläfli, Salmon,
Clifford, Krönecker, have an inner assurance of the reality of transcendental space, I strive to bring my faculties of mental vision into
accordance with theirs. The positive evidence in such cases is
more worthy than the negative, and actuality is not cancelled or
balanced by privation, as matter plus space is none the less matter.
I acknowledge two separate sources of authority—the collective
sense of mankind, and the illumination of privileged intellects.
As a parallel case, I would ask whether it is by demonstrative
processes that the doctrine of limits and of infinitely greats
and smalls, has found its way to the ready acceptance of the
multitude; or whether, after deducting whatever may be due
to modified hereditary cerebral organisation, it is not a consequence rather of the insensible moulding of the ideas under the
influence of language which has become permeated with the
notions originating in the minds of a few great thinkers? I am
assured that Germans, even of the non-literary class, such as
ladies of fashion and novel readers, are often appalled by the
hebetude of their English friends in muddling up together, as
if they were nearly or quite the same thing, the reason and the
understanding, In doing into English the words Vernunft and
Verstand, thereby confounding distinctions now become familiar

age, and with happy consequences, the same bold hypothesis.

Most, if not all, of the great ideas of modern mathematics have had their origin in observation. Take, for instance, the arithmetical theory of forms, of which the foundation was laid in the diophantine theorems of Fermat, left without proof by their author, which resisted all the efforts of the myriad-minded Euler to reduce to demonstration, and only yielded up their cause of being when turned over in the blowpipe flame of Gauss's transcendent genius; or the doctrine of double periodicity, which resulted from the observation by Jacobi of a purely analytical fact of transformation; or Legendre's law of reciprocity; or Sturm's theorem about the roots of equations, which, as he informed me with his own lips, stared him in the face in the midst of some mechanical investigations connected with the motion of compound pendulums; or Huyghen's method of continued fractions, characterized by Lagrange as one of the principal discoveries of 'that great mathematician, and to which he appears to have been led by the con-

(such is the force of language) to the very milkmaids of Fatherland.

As a public teacher of mere striplings, I am often amazed by the facility and absence of resistance with which the principles of the infinitesimal calculus are accepted and assimilated by the present race of learners. When I was young, a boy of sixteen or seventeen who knew his infinitesimal calculus would have been almost pointed at in the streets as a prodigy, like Dante, as a man who had seen hell. Now-a-days, our Woolwich cadets at the same age, talk with glee of tangents and asymptotes and points of contrary flexure and discuss questions of double maxima and minima, or ballistic pendulums, or motion in a resisting medium, under the familiar and ignoble name of *sums*.

struction of his Planetary Automaton;' or the New Algebra, speaking of which one of my predecessors (Mr. Spottiswoode) has said, not without just reason and authority, from this chair, 'that it reaches out and indissolubly connects itself each year with fresh branches of mathematics, that the theory of equations has almost become new through it, algebraic geometry transfigured in its light, that the calculus of variations, molecular physics, and mechanics' (he might, if speaking at the present moment, go on to add the theory of elasticity and the highest developments of the integral calculus) 'have all felt its influence.'

Now, this gigantic outcome of modern analytical thought, itself, too, only the precursor and progenitor of a future still more heaven-reaching theory, which will comprise a complete study of the interoperation, the actions and reactions, of algebraic forms (Analytical Morphology in its absolute sense), how did this originate? In the accidental observation by Eisenstein, some score or more years ago, of a single invariant (the Quadrinvariant of a Binary Quartic) which he met with in the course of certain researches just as accidentally and unexpectedly as M. Du Chaillu might meet a gorilla in the country of the Fantees, or any one of us in London a white polar bear escaped from the Zoological Gardens. Fortunately he pounced down upon his prey and preserved it for the contemplation and study of future mathematicians. It occupies only part of a page in his collected posthumous works. This single result of observation (as well entitled to be so called as the discovery of Globigerinae in chalk or of the confoco-ellipsoidal structure of the shells of the Foraminifera), which remained unproductive in the hands of its distinguished author, has served to set in motion a train of thought and to propagate an impulse which have led to a complete revolution in the whole aspect of modern analysis, and whose consequences will continue to be felt until Mathematics are forgotten and British Associations meet no more.

I might go on, were it necessary, piling instance upon instance, to prove the paramount importance of the faculty of observation to the progress of mathematical discovery.* Were it not unbecoming to dilate on one's personal experience, I could tell a story of almost romantic interest about my own latest researches in a field where Geometry, Algebra, and the Theory of Numbers melt in a surprising manner into one another, like sunset tints or the colours of the dying dolphin, 'the last still loveliest,' a sketch of which has just appeared in the Proceedings of the London Mathematical Society†), which would very strikingly illustrate how much observation, divination, induction, experimental trial, and verification, causation, too (if that means, as I suppose

---

* Newton's Rule (subsequently and for the first time reduced by myself to demonstration in No. 2 of the London Mathematical Society's Proceedings) was to all appearance, and according to the more received opinion, obtained inductively by its author. So also my reduction of Euler's problem of the Virgins (or rather one slightly more general than this) to the form of a question (or, to speak more exactly, a set of questions) in simple partitions was (strangely enough) first obtained by myself inductively, the result communicated to Prof. Cayley, and proved subsequently by each of us independently, and by perfectly distinct methods.

† Under the title of *Outline Trace of the Theory of Reducible Cyclodes*.

it must, mounting from phenomena to their reasons or causes of being), have to do with the work of the mathematician. In the face of these facts, which every analyst in this room or out of it can vouch for out of his own knowledge and personal experience, how can it be maintained, in the words of Professor Huxley, who, in this instance, is speaking of the sciences as they are in themselves and without any reference to scholastic discipline, that Mathematics 'is that study which knows nothing of observation, nothing of induction, nothing of experiment, nothing of causation.'*

* Induction and analogy are the special characteristics of modern mathematics, in which theorems have given place to theories, and no truth is regarded otherwise than as a link in an infinite chain. 'Omne exit in infinitum' is their favourite motto and accepted axiom. No mathematician now-a-days sets any store on the discovery of isolated theorems, except as affording hints of an unsuspected new sphere of thought, like meteorites detached from some undiscovered planetary orb of speculation. The form, as well as matter, of mathematical science, as must be the case in any true living organic science, is in a constant state of flux, and the position of its centre of gravity is liable to continual change. At different periods in its history defined, with more or less accuracy, as the science of number or quantity, or extension or operation or arrangement, it appears at present to be passing through a phase in which the development of the notion of Continuity plays the leading part. In exemplification of the generalising tendency of modern mathematics, take so simple a fact as that of two straight lines or two planes being incapable of including 'a space.' When analysed this statement will be found to resolve itself into the assertion that if two out of the four triads that can be formed with four points lie respectively *in directo*, the same must be true of the remaining two triads; and that if two of the five tetrads that can be formed with five points lie respectively *in plano*, the remaining three tetrads (subject to a certain obvious exception) must each do the same. This, at least, is one way of arriving at the notion

I, of course, am not so absurd as to maintain that the habit of observation of external nature* will be best or in any degree cultivated by the study of mathematics, at all events as that study is at present conducted, and no one can desire more earnestly than myself to see natural and experimental science introduced into our schools as a primary and indispensable branch of

of an unlimited rectilinear and planar schema of points. The two statements above made, translated into the language of determinants, immediately suggest as their generalised expression my great 'Homaloidal Law,' which affirms that the vanishing of a certain specifiable number of minor determinants of a given order of any matrix (i.e. rectangular array of quantities) implies the simultaneous evanescence of all the rest of that order. I made (inter alia) a beautiful application of this law (which is, I believe, recorded in Mr. Spottiswoode's valuable treatise on Determinants, but where besides I know not) to the establishment of the well-known relations, wrung out with so much difficulty by Euler, between the cosines of the nine angles, which two sets of rectangular axes in space make with one another. This is done by contriving and constructing a matrix such that the six known equations connecting the nine cosines taken both ways in sets of threes shall be expressed by the evanescence of six of its minors; the simultaneous evanescence of the remaining minors given by the Homaloidal Law will then be found to express the relations in question (which Euler has put on record, it drove him almost to despair to obtain), but which are thus obtained by a simple process of inspection and reading off, without any labour whatever. The fact that such a law, containing in a latent form so much refined algebra, and capable of such interesting immediate applications, should present itself to the *observation* merely as the extended expression of the ground of the possibility of our most elementary and seemingly intuitive conceptions concerning the right line and plane, has often filled me with amazement to reflect upon.

* As the prerogative of Natural Science is to cultivate a taste for observation, so that of Mathematics is, almost from the starting-point, to stimulate the faculty of invention.

education: I think that that study and mathematical culture should go on hand in hand together, and that they would greatly influence each other for their mutual good. I should rejoice to see mathematics taught with that life and animation which the presence and example of her young and buoyant sister could not fail to impart, short roads preferred to long ones, Euclid honourably shelved or buried 'deeper than e'er plummet sounded' out of the schoolboy's reach, morphology introduced into the elements of Algebra—projection, correlation, and motion accepted as aids to geometry—the mind of the student quickened and elevated and his faith awakened by early initiation into the ruling ideas of polarity, continuity, infinity, and familiarization with the doctrine of the imaginary and inconceivable.

It is this living interest in the subject which is so wanting in our traditional and mediaeval modes of teaching. In France, Germany, and Italy, everywhere where I have been on the Continent, mind acts direct on mind in a manner unknown to the frozen formality of our academic institutions; schools of thought and centres of real intellectual co-operation exist; the relation of master and pupil is acknowledged as a spiritual and a lifelong tie, connecting successive generations of great thinkers with each other in an unbroken chain, just in the same way as we read in the catalogue of our French Exhibition, or of the Salon at Paris, of this man or that being the pupil of one great painter or sculptor and the master of another. When followed out in this spirit, there is no study in the world which brings into more harmonious action all the faculties of the mind than the one of which I stand here as the humble representative, there is none other which prepares so many agreeable surprises for its followers, more wonderful than the changes in the transformation-scene of a pantomime, or, like this, seems to raise them, by successive steps of initiation, to higher and higher states of conscious intellectual being.

This accounts, I believe, for the extraordinary longevity of all the greatest masters of the analytical art, the dii majores of the mathematical Pantheon. Leibnitz lived to the age of 70; Euler to 76; Lagrange to 77; Laplace to 78; Gauss to 78; Plato, the supposed inventor of the conic sections, who made mathematics his study and delight, who called them the handles (or aids) to philosophy, the medicine of the soul, and is said never to have let a day go by without inventing some new theorems, lived to 82; Newton, the crown and glory of his race, to 85; Archimedes, the nearest akin, probably, to Newton in genius, was 75, and might have lived on to be 100, for aught we can guess to the contrary, when he was slain by the impatient and ill-mannered sergeant, sent to bring him before the Roman general, in the full vigour of his faculties, and in the very act of working out a problem; Pythagoras, in whose school, I believe, the word mathematician (used, however, in a somewhat wider than its present sense) originated, the second founder of geometry, the inventor of the matchless theorem which goes by his name, the precognizer of the undoubtedly mis-called Copernican theory, the discoverer of the regular solids and the musical canon, who stands at the very apex of this pyramid of flame (if we may credit the tradition), after spending 22 years studying in Egypt, and 12 in Babylon, opened school when 56 or 57 years old in Magna Graecia, married a young wife when past 60, and died, carrying on his work with energy unspent to the last, at the age of 99. The mathematician lives long and lives young; the wings of his soul do not early drop off, nor do its pores become clogged with the earthy particles blown from the dusty highways of vulgar life.

Some people have been found to regard all mathematics, after the 47th proposition of the first book of Euclid, as a sort of morbid secretion, to be compared only with the pearl said to be generated in the diseased oyster, or, as I have heard it described, 'une excroissance maladive de l'esprit humain.' Others find its justification, its 'raison d'être,' in its being either the torch-bearer leading the way, or the handmaiden holding up the train of Physical Science; and a very clever writer in a recent magazine article, expresses his doubts whether it is, in itself, a more serious pursuit, or more worthy or interesting an intellectual human being, than the study of chess problems or Chinese puzzles.* What is it to us, they say, if the three angles of a triangle are equal to two right angles, or if every even number is, or may be, the sum of two primes,† or if every equation of an

* Is it not the same disregard of principles, the same indifference to truth for its own sake which prompts the question, 'Where's the good of it?' in reference to speculative science, and 'Where's the harm of it?' in reference to white lies and pious frauds? In my own experience I have found that the very same class of people who delight to put the first question are in the habit of acting upon the denial implied in the second. *Abit in mores incuria.*

† This theorem still awaits proof; it is stated, I believe, in

odd degree must have a real root? How dull, stale, flat, and unprofitable are such and such like announcements! Much more interesting to read an account of a marriage in high life, or the details of an international boat-race. But this is like judging of architecture from being shown some of the brick and mortar, or even a quarried stone, of a public building, or of painting from the colours mixed on the palette, or of music by listening to the thin and screechy sounds produced by a bow passed haphazard over the strings of a violin. The world of ideas which it discloses or illuminates, the contemplation of divine beauty and order which it induces, the harmonious connection of its parts, the infinite hierarchy and absolute evidence of the truths with which it is concerned, these, and such like, are

Euler's correspondence with Goldbach: I re-discovered it in ignorance of Euler's having mentioned it, in connection with a theory of my own concerning cubic forms. The evidence in its favour is *induction* of the undemonstrative or purely accumulative kind, and it may or may not turn out eventually to be true. As a most learned scholar who heard this address given at Exeter remarked to me, not many days ago, it is certainly by no process of deduction that we make out that five times six is thirty. I mention this, because I know some, who agree, or did agree, with Professor Huxley's published opinions about mathematics, are under the impression that the higher processes of mind in mathematics only concern 'the aristocracy of mathematicians:' on the contrary, they lie at the very foundations of the subject. There are besides, and in abundance, mathematical processes which only by a forced interpretation can be brought under the head of demonstration, whether deductive or inductive, and really belong to a sort of artistic and constructive faculty, such for example as evaluating definite integrals, or making out the best way one can the number of distinct branches and the general character of each branch of a curve from its algebraical equation.

the surest grounds of the title of mathematics to human regard, and would remain unimpeached and unimpaired were the plan of the universe unrolled like a map at our feet, and the mind of man qualified to take in the whole scheme of creation at a glance.

In conformity with general usage, I have employed the word mathematics in the plural; but I think it would be desirable that this form of word should be reserved for the applications of the science, and that we should use Mathematic in the singular number to denote the science itself, in the same way as we speak of logic, rhetoric, or (own sister to algebra *) music. Time was when all parts of the subject were dissevered, when algebra, geometry, and arithmetic either lived apart or kept up cold relations of acquaintance confined to occasional calls upon one another; but that state of things is now happily at an end; they are drawn together and are constantly becoming more and more intimately related and connected by a thousand fresh ties, and we may confidently look forward to a time when they shall form but one body with one soul. Geometry formerly was the chief borrower from arithmetic and algebra, but it has since repaid its obligations with abundant usury; and if I were asked to name, in one word, the pole-star round which the mathe-

* I have elsewhere (in my Trilogy, published in the *Philosophical Transactions*) referred to the close connection between these two cultures, not merely as having Arithmetic for their common parent, but as similar in their habits and affections. I have called 'Music the Algebra of sense, Algebra the Music of the reason; Music the dream, Algebra the waking life—the soul of each the same!'

matical firmament revolves, the central idea which pervades as a hidden spirit the whole corpus of mathematical doctrine, I should point to Continuity as contained in our notions of space, and say, it is this, it is this! Space is the *Grand Continuum* from which, as from an inexhaustible reservoir, all the fertilizing ideas of modern analysis are derived; and as Brindley, the engineer, once allowed before a parliamentary committee that, in his opinion, rivers were made to feed navigable canals, I feel almost tempted to say that one principal reason for the existence of space, or at least one principal function which it discharges, is that of feeding mathematical invention. Everybody knows what a wonderful influence geometry has exercised in the hands of Cauchy, Puiseux, Riemann, and his followers Clebsch, Gordan, and others, over the very form and presentment of the modern calculus, and how it has come to pass that the tracing of curves, which was at one time to be regarded as a puerile amusement, or at best useful only to the architect or decorator, is now entitled to take rank as a high philosophical exercise, inasmuch as every new curve or surface, or other circumscription of space, is capable of being regarded as the embodiment of some specific organised system of Continuity.*

* M. Camille Jordan's application of Dr. Salmon's Eikosiheptagram to Abelian functions is one of the most recent instances of this reverse action of geometry on analysis. Mr. Crofton's admirable apparatus of a reticulation with infinitely fine meshes rotated successively through indefinitely small angles, which he applies to obtaining whole families of definite integrals, is another equally striking example of the same phenomenon. I am happy to be able to add that this gentleman who, when the above lines were printed, was at the bottom of

The early study of Euclid made me a hater of geometry, which I hope may plead my excuse if I have shocked the opinions of any in this room (and I know there are some who rank Euclid as second in sacredness to the Bible alone, and as one of the advanced outposts of the British Constitution) by the tone in which I have previously alluded to it as a school-book; and yet, in spite of this repugnance, which had become a second nature in me, whenever I went far enough into any mathematical question, I found I touched, at last, a geometrical bottom; so it was, I may instance, in the purely arithmetical theory of partitions; so, again, in one of my more recent studies, the purely algebraical question of the invariantive criteria of the nature of the roots of an equation of the fifth degree: the first inquiry landed me in a new theory of polyhedra; the latter found its perfect and only possible complete * solu-

---

the Staff of the Mathematical Instructors at Woolwich, has been since appointed, with the full concurrence of his colleagues, on the nomination of the Governor, Sir John Lintorn Simmons, K.C.B., to succeed me as Professor of Mathematics at the Royal Military Academy.

* *Complete* in the sense of *universal*, more *than perfect or complete* in the ordinary sense. Two criteria are absolutely fixed; but in addition to these two an additional criterion or set of criteria must be introduced to make the system of conditions sufficient. The number of such set may be either one or whatever number we please, and into such one or into each of the set (if more than one) an indefinite number of arbitrary parameters (limited) may be introduced. Now the geometrical construction I arrive at contains implicitly the totality of all these infinitely varied forms of criteria, or sets of criteria, and without it the existence and possibility of such variety in the shape of the solution could never have been anticipated or understood. My truly eminent friend M. Charles Hermite (Membre de l'Institut), with all the efforts of his extraordinary analytical power, and

tion in the construction of a surface of the ninth order, and the sub-division of its infinite contents into three distinct natural regions.*

Having thus expressed myself at much greater length than I originally intended on the subject, which, as

with the knowledge of my results to guide him, has only been able by the non-geometrical method to arrive at one form of solution consisting of a third criterion absolutely definite and destitute of a single variable parameter. As is well known, I have made a very important use of a criterion of the same form as M. Hermite's, but containing one arbitrary parameter (limited). The subject will be found resumed from the point where I left it, and pursued in considerable detail by Prof. Cayley, in one of his more recent memoirs on Quartics in the 'Philosophical Transactions.' M. Hermite it was who first surprised Invariantists (l'Eglise Invariantive, as we are sometimes styled) by an *à priori* demonstration that the nature of the roots or factors of quartics could in general be found by means of invariantive criteria. This was known to be possible up to the *fourth* order of binary quartics, and impossible for the *fourth*. M. Hermite showed that this negation which seemed to stop the way to further progress was an exceptional case; that whereas for the second, third, fifth, sixth, and all higher degrees the thing could be done, for the fourth alone it was impossible: as regards linear Quantics, the question does not arise. I look upon this failure of a law for one term in the middle of an infinite progression as an unparalleled *miracle of arithmetic*, far more real and deeper seated than the one alluded to by Mr. Babbage in connection with the discontinuous action of a supposed machine in his ninth Bridgwater Treatise.

* So I found, as a pure matter of observation, that allineation (*alignement*) in ornamental gardening—i.e. the method of putting trees in positions to form a very great number or the greatest number possible of straight rows, of which a few special cases only had been previously considered as detached porismatic problems, forms part of a great connected theory of the pluperfect points on a cubic curve, those points, of which the nine points of Inflection and Plücker's twenty-seven points may serve as the lowest instances.

standing first on the muster-roll of the Association, and as having been so recently and repeatedly arraigned before the bar of public opinion, is entitled to be heard in its defence (if anywhere) in this place,—having endeavoured to show what it is not, what it is, and what it is probably destined to become, I feel that I must enough and more than enough, have trespassed on your forbearance, and shall proceed with the regular business of the meeting.

Before calling upon the authors of the papers contained in the varied bill of intellectual fare which I see before me, I hope to be pardoned if I direct attention to the importance of practising brevity and condensation in the delivery of communications to the Section, not merely as a saving of valuable time, but in order that what is said may be more easily followed and listened to with greater pleasure and advantage. I believe that immense good may be done by the oral interchange and discussion of ideas which takes place in the Sections; but for this to be possible, details and long descriptions should be reserved for printing and reading, and only the general outlines and broad statements of facts, methods, observations, or inventions brought before us here, such as can be easily followed by persons having a fair average acquaintance with the several subjects treated upon. I understand the rule to be that, with the exception of the author of any paper who may answer questions and reply at the end of the discussion, no member is to address the Section more than once on the same subject, or occupy more than a quarter of an hour in speaking.

In order to get through the business set down in each day's paper, it may sometimes be necessary for me to bring a discussion to an earlier close than might otherwise be desirable, and for that purpose to request the authors of papers, and those who speak upon them, to be brief in their addresses. I have known most able investigators at these meetings, and especially in this section, gradually part company with their audience, and at last become so involved in digressions as to lose entirely the thread of their discourse, and seem to forget, like men waking out of sleep, where they were or what they were talking about. In such cases I shall venture to give a gentle pull to the string of the kite before it soars right away out of sight into the region of the clouds. I now call upon Dr. Magnus to read his paper and recount to the Section his wondrous story on the Emission, Absorption, and Reflection of Obscure Heat.*

POSTSCRIPT.—The remarks on the use of experimental methods in mathematical investigation led to Dr. Jacobi, the eminent physicist of St. Petersburg, who was present at the delivery of the address, favouring me with the annexed anecdote relative to his illustrious brother C. G. J. Jacobi.†

* Curiously enough, and as if symptomatic of the genial warmth of the proceedings in which seven sages from distant lands (Jacobi, Magnus, Newton, Janssen, Morren, Lyman, Neumayer) took frequent part, the opening and concluding papers (each of surpassing interest, and a letting-out of mighty waters) were on Obscure Heat, by Prof. Magnus, and on Stellar Heat, by Mr. Huggins.

† It is said of Jacobi, that he attracted the particular attention and friendship of Böckh, the director of the philological seminary at Berlin, by the zeal and talent he displayed for philology, and only at the end of two years' study at the University, and

'En causant un jour avec mon frère défunt sur la nécessité de contrôler par des expériences réitérées toute observation, même si elle confirme l'hypothèse, il me raconta avoir découvert un jour une loi très-remarquable de la théorie des nombres, dont il ne douta guère qu'elle fût générale. Cependant par un excès de précaution ou plutôt pour faire le superflu, il voulut substituer un chiffre quelconque réel aux termes généraux, chiffre qu'il choisit au hasard ou, peut-être, par une espèce de divination, car en effet ce chiffre mit sa formule en défaut; tout autre chiffre qu'il essaya en confirma la généralité. Plus tard il réussit à prouver que le chiffre choisi par lui par hasard, appartenait à un système de chiffres qui faisait la seule exception à la règle.

'Ce fait curieux m'est resté dans la mémoire, mais comme il s'est passé il y a plus d'une trentaine d'années, je ne rappelle plus des détails.

'M. H. Jacobi.'

'Exeter, 24 août, 1869.'

after a severe mental struggle, was able to make his final choice in favour of mathematics. The relation between these two sciences is not perhaps so remote as may at first sight appear; and indeed it has often struck me that metamorphosis runs like a golden thread through the most diverse branches of modern intellectual culture, and forms a natural link of connection between subjects in their aims so remote as grammar, philology, ethnology, rational mythology, chemistry, botany, comparative anatomy, physiology, physics, algebra, versification, music, all of which, under the modern point of view, may be regarded as having morphology for their common centre. Even singing, I have been told, the advanced German theorists regard as being strictly a development of recitative, and infer therefrom that no essentially new melodic themes can be invented until a social cataclysm, or the civilisation of some at present barbaric races, shall have created fresh necessities of expression, and called into activity new forms of impassioned declamation.

APPENDIX.

ON THE INCORRECT DESCRIPTION OF KANT'S DOCTRINE OF SPACE AND TIME COMMON IN ENGLISH WRITERS.[*]

In the very remarkable contribution by Professor Sylvester (*Nature*, No. 9) this sentence occurs: 'It is very common, not to say universal, with English writers, even such authorised ones as Whewell, Lewes, or Herbert Spencer, to refer to Kant's doctrine as affirming space to be a "form of thought" "or of the understanding." This is putting into Kant's mouth (as pointed out to me by Dr. C. M. Ingleby) words which he would have been the first to disclaim.'

It is not on personal grounds that I wish to rectify the misconception into which Dr. Ingleby has betrayed Professor Sylvester. When objections are made to what I have written, it is my habit either silently to correct my error, or silently to disregard the criticism. In the present case I might be perfectly contented to disregard a criticism which any one who even glanced at my exposition of Kant would see to be altogether inexact; but as misapprehensions of Kant are painfully abundant, readers of Kant being few, and those who take his name in vain being many, it may be worth while to stop *this* error from getting into circulation through the channel of *Nature*. Kant assuredly did teach, as Professor Sylvester says, and as I have repeatedly stated, that space is a form of intuition. But there is no discrepancy at all in also saying that he taught space to be a 'form of thought,' since every student of Kant knows that intuition without thought is mere sensuous *impression*. Kant considered the mind under three

[*] From *Nature*. See note [*], p. 109.

aspects, Sensibility, Understanding, and Reason. The *à priori* forms of Sensibility, which rendered Experience possible, were Space and Time: these were forms of thought, conditions of cognition. It was by such forms of thought that he reoccupied the position taken by Leibnitz in defending and amending the doctrine of innate ideas, namely, that knowledge has another source besides sensible experience—the *intellectus ipse*.

While, therefore, any one who spoke of space as a 'form of the understanding' would certainly use language which Kant would have disclaimed, Kant himself would have been surprised to hear that space was not held by him as a 'form of thought.'

January 3. GEORGE HENRY LEWES.

THE following paragraphs, I believe, faithfully render sundry passages of Kant's writings:—

'Objects are given to us by means of sense (Sinnlichkeit), which is the sole source of intuitions (Anschauungen); but they are thought by the understanding, from which arise conceptions (Begriffe).' ('Kritik,' p. 53, Hartenstein's edition.)

'The understanding is the faculty of thought. Thought is knowledge by means of conception.' (*Ibid.* p. 93.)

'The original consciousness of space is an intuition *à priori*, and not a conception (Begriff).' (*Ibid.* p. 60.)

'Space is nothing else than the form of all the phenomena of the external senses; that is, it is the subjective condition of sense, under which alone external intuition is possible for us.' (*Ibid.* p. 61.)

'Our nature is such, that intuition can never be otherwise than sensual (sinnlich); that is, it only contains the modes in which we are affected by objects. On the other hand, the power of thinking the object of sensual intuition, is the understanding. Neither of these faculties is superior to the other. Without sense, no object would be given us, and without understanding none would be thought. Thoughts without contents are empty, intuitions without conceptions (Begriffe) are blind.' (*Ibid.* p. 62.)

'Time and space are "mere forms of sense"' (Formen unserer Sinnlichkeit, 'Prolegomena,' p. 33) and 'mere forms of intuition.' ('Kritik,' p. 76.)

With these passages before one, there can be no doubt that that thorough and acute student of Kant, Dr. Ingleby, was perfectly right when he said that Kant would have repudiated the affirmation that 'space is a form of thought.' For in these sentences, and in many others which might be cited, Kant expressly lays down the doctrine that thought is the work of the understanding, intuition of the sense; and that space, like time, is an intuition. The only 'forms of thought' in Kant's sense, are the categories. T. H. HUXLEY.

January 14.

I DO not believe Professor Sylvester has been betrayed, as Mr. G. H. Lewes asserts, into any misconception of this matter by me.

When Kant, at the outset, says, 'Alles Denken aber muss sich, es sei geradezu oder im Umschweife, vermittelst gewisser Merkmale, zuletzt auf Anschauungen...beziehen,' it would take the veriest dunderhead not to see that all forms of intuition must be, indirectly at least, forms of thought. I never dreamed of disputing so obvious a position. But I object to the phrase, 'forms of thought,' as designating Space and Time, on the ground of precision. They are *peculiarly* forms of general Sense, and not forms of Thought *as Thought*. Kant, I believe, eschewed the phrase in that sense, and, for all I see, might for the same reason have disclaimed it. C. M. INGLEBY.

Ilford, Jan. 14.

IT is not my habit 'when objections are made to what I have written, silently to correct my error or silently disregard the criticism.' If the objections are well founded, I think it due to the cause of truth to make a frank confession of error, and in the opposite case to reply to the objections.

With reference, then, to Mr. Lewes's strictures in *Nature's* last number, I beg to say that Dr. Ingleby has 'betrayed' me into no error. If I have fallen into error, it is with my eyes open, and after satisfying myself by study of Kant, that to speak of Space and Time, whether as forms of understanding, or as forms of thought, is an unauthorised and misleading mode of expression. Space and Time are forms of sensitivity or intuition. The categories of Kant (so essentially in this point differing from those of Aristotle) do not contain Space and Time among them, and are properly called forms of understanding or thought.

To the existence of thought the operation of the understanding is a necessary preliminary.

Sensibility and intuition are antecedent to any such operation.

Can Mr. Lewes point to any passage in Kant where Space and Time are designated *forms of thought*? I shall indeed be surprised if he can do so—as much surprised as if Mr. Todhunter or Mr. Routh, in their Mechanical Treatises, were to treat *energy* and *force* as convertible terms. To such a misuse of the word energy it would be little to the point to urge that *force without energy is a mere potential tendency*. It is just as little to the point in the matter at issue, for Mr. Lewes to inform the readers of *Nature* that *intuition without thought is mere sensuous impression*.

Dr. Ingleby has rendered, in my opinion, a very great service to the English reading public, by drawing attention to so serious and prevalent an error as that of confounding the categories (the proper forms of thought *as thought*) with Space and Time, the forms of intuition, the sentinels, so to say, who keep watch and ward outside the gates of the Understanding.

Athenaeum Club, Jan. 15.   J. J. SYLVESTER.

ALTHOUGH I do not feel myself called upon to modify in the least what was said in my former letter on this subject, the three letters which appear to-day in answer to it are too important to be left unnoticed.

The case is briefly this: In the 'History of Philosophy' I had to expound Kant's doctrine, and to criticise it, not only in itself, but in reference to the great question of the origin of knowledge. In the pages of exposition I *uniformly* speak of Space and Time as forms of Intuition; no language can be plainer. I also mark the distinction between Sensibility and Understanding, as that of Intuition and Thought. After enumerating the Categories, I add, 'In those Categories Kant finds the pure forms of the Understanding. They render Thought possible.'

But when, ceasing to expound the system, I had to criticise it, and especially to consider it in reference to the great question; there was no longer any need to adhere to a mode of expression which would have been obscure and misleading. I therefore *uniformly* class Space and Time *among the forms of Thought*, connecting them with the doctrine of Necessary Truths and Fundamental Ideas, which, according to the *à priori* school, are furnished ready-made—brought by the Mind as its native dowry, not evolved in it through Experience.

Now the question is, Have I put language into Kant's mouth which he would disclaim, or is such language misleading? That Kant would have said the language was not what he had employed, I freely admit; but that he would have disclaimed it as misrepresenting his meaning, I deny. I was not bound to follow his language when the task of exposition was at an end; but only bound not to translate his opinions into language which would distort them.

In classing Space and Time *among* the Forms of Thought, I classed them *beside* the Categories of the Understanding and the Ideas of Reason, i.e. the purely intellectual conditions existing *à priori* in the Mind. The Mind is said by Kant to be endowed with three faculties—Sensibility, Understanding, and Reason. The activity of the Mind is threefold—Intuitive Thought, Conceptive or Discursive Thought, and Regulative Thought. There could not be an equivoque in my using the word Thought in its ordinary philosophical acceptation as expressive of all mental activity whatever, exclusive of mere sensation; although Kant assigns a more restricted meaning in his technical use of the word, i.e. what we call Logic. And that Kant *meant* nothing opposed to the ordinary interpretation is obvious. It is obvious because, as I said in my former letter, Intuition without Thought is mere sensuous impression. Mr. Sylvester demurs to this, so I will show it in a single citation:—'In the transcendental Aesthetic,' says Kant, 'we will first isolate Sensibility by separating from it all that the Understanding through its concepts thinks therewith, so that nothing but empirical Intuition remains. Secondly, we will lop off from this empirical Intuition everything relating to sensation (*Empfindung*); so that thereby nothing will remain but pure Intuition and the mere form of phenomena, which is the one thing that Sensibility can furnish *à priori*. By this investigation it will appear that there are two pure forms of sensuous Intuition which are *à priori* principles of Cognition.' ('Kritik,' § 1, ed. Hartenstein, p. 61.)

Mr. Sylvester correctly says, that Intuition and Thought are not convertible terms. But he is incorrect in assuming that they differ as potential and actual; they differ as species and genus; therefore, whatever is a form of Intuition, though not a form of Logic, must be a form of Thought; unless intuitive Thought be denied altogether. How little Kant denied it is evident in every section of his work. In asserting that Space and Time as Intuitions belong to the subjective constitution of the Mind—*subjectiven Beschaffenheit unseres Gemüths* (p. 62)—he expresses this; but it is unequivocally expressed in the following definition:—'A perception, when it refers solely to the subject, as a modification of its states, is *sensation*, an objective perception is *cognition*: *this is either Intuition or Concept*, "intuitus vel conceptus."' ('Kritik,' p. 294.) Is not thought implied in cognition? Again:—'The proposition "I think" is an undetermined empirical Intuition, i.e. Perception consequently, it proves that Sensation, which belongs to Sensibility, must lie at the basis of this proposition. . . . I do not mean thereby that the "I" in the "I think" is an empirical representation (*Vorstellung*), on the contrary, it is *purely intellectual, because it belongs to thought in general*. But without some empirical representation which would give Thought its material there could be no such act of Thought as the "I think"' (p. 324, *note*).

'Man is always thinking,' says Hegel, 'even when he has nothing but intuitions'—*denkend ist der Mensch immer auch wenn er nur anschaut.*' (Encyclop. § 24.)

If, because Kant has a restricted use of the term Thought, all who venture on the more ordinary use are said to misrepresent his philosophical meaning, I must call upon those who criticise this laxity to refrain henceforth from speaking of Reason as Thought, since Kant no less excluded Reason from the province of the Understanding. If 'the only forms of thought, in Kant's sense, are the Categories,' this sweeps away Reason on the one side, as it sweeps away Sensibility on the other; and Ideas are not more correctly named Thoughts than Intuitions are. Kant, it is true, speaks of the concepts of Reason, and defines an Idea to be a 'Vernunftbegriff' (page 294); but Kant, equally and in a hundred places, speaks of the 'concept of Space' (Begriff des Raumes). The truth is, as already intimated, that in spite of his technical restriction of Thought to the formation of concepts, he recognised intuitive and regulative Thought no less than discursive Thought; nor would his system have had any coherence without such a recognition. Why does he call his work the 'Critik of Pure Reason,' unless he intended to display the common intellectual ground of Sensibility, Understanding, and Reason? and does not the word Thought, in ordinary philosophical language mean this activity of the Intellect? When, by Sir W. Hamilton, Dr. Whewell, Mr. Spencer, and myself, the phrase Forms of Thought is used, does not every reader understand it as meaning Forms of intellectual activity?

In conclusion, I affirm that in the ordinary acceptation of the term Thought—the activity of the Mind—Space and Time as forms of Intuition are forms of Thought, conditions of mental action; and to suppose that because Kant's language is different, his meaning is misrepresented by classing forms of Intuition among the forms of Thought is to misunderstand Kant's doctrine and its purpose.   GEORGE HENRY LEWES.

January 22.

Dr. INGLEBY, I should think, is quite entitled to say not only that Kant might, but that he would, have disclaimed the phrase Form of Thought as applied to Space or Time taken simply. The remark of Mr. Lewes, that 'intuition without thought is mere sensuous impression,'—or, as it might have been put, that phenomena of sense (constituted such in the forms of Space and Time) must further be thought under Categories of Understanding, before they can be said to be known or to become intellectual experience—cannot be a sufficient reason for making a Form of Thought proper out of a Form of Intuition.

There is, nevertheless (and Mr. Lewes does not fail to suggest it), a sense in which, when taken along with the Categories of the Understanding, and with or without the Ideas of the Reason, the Forms of Intuition may be spoken of as Forms of Thought: Thought being understood, with the same extension that Kant himself gives to Reason in the title (not the body) of his work, as equivalent to faculty of Knowledge in general. It is in this sense that Kant calls all the forms alike, à *priori* principles of Knowledge; and the ambiguity of the word Thought is so well recognised that the English writers arraigned by Prof. Sylvester take no great liberty, when for their purpose, which commonly is the discussion of the general question as to the origin of Knowledge, they talk generally of Kant's 'Forms of Thought.' If, indeed, any of them ever speaks of Space as a 'form of the Understanding,' which was part of the original charge, the case is very different; Kant being so careful with his *Verstand.* But Mr. Lewes, at least, would never be caught speaking thus, even though his main reason for merging Intuition in Thought might seem to justify this also.   G. CROOM ROBERTSON.

University College, January 22.

You will perhaps permit me to make a remark on a controversy at present going on in your columns. There has seldom, I believe, been a grosser or more misleading perversion of the Critical Philosophy than ascribing to Kant the view that Space and Time are in any meaning of the terms 'forms of thought.'

One of his chief grounds of complaint against Leibnitz is, that the latter 'intellectualised these forms of the sensibility' (Meiklejohn's translation of the 'Critick,' p. 108): and lest the import of this assertion should be mistaken, he explicitly tells us that 'Space and Time are not merely forms of sensuous intuition, but intuitions themselves' (Meiklejohn's trans., p. 98): that is, *sensuous* intuitions, as he has been just before asserting that all human intuitions must be. It is precisely on this distinction of pure sensibility and pure thought that Kant founds the possibility of Mathematics—a science which could never be derived from a mere analysis of the concepts employed, but only from the construction of them in intuition. He ridicules, for example, the idea of attempting to deduce the proposition, 'Two right lines cannot enclose a space,' from the mere concepts or notions of a straight line and the number two. 'All your endeavours,' says he, 'are in vain, and you find yourself compelled to have recourse to intuition, as in fact Geometry always does.' (Meiklejohn, p. 39: see also his long contrast of Mathematical and dogmatical methods in the beginning of the 'Methodology.') And not only is Kant's Mathematical theory founded on this distinction, but his Physical theory also, since it is only by means of pure intuition that he connects pure thought with sensations (see the 'Schematism,' and still more the 'General Remark on the System of Principles,' Meiklejohn, pp. 174-7); and when he fails to make out this connection he regards the Ideas of Pure Reason as possessed of no objective validity (Transcendental Dialectic). In the first edition of the 'Critick' he went still further, and in his remarks on the Second Paralogism of Rational Psychology he speaks of 'that something which lies at the basis of external phenomena, which so *affects* our *sense* as to give it the representations of *space*, matter, *form*, &c.' And while he abbreviated his discussion in the second edition, he tells us in his preface that he found nothing to alter in the views put forward in the previous one.

I might quote whole pages of the 'Critick' in proof of these views, but I ought rather to apologise for writing so much after the letters which you have already published. I believe the mistaken as to Kant's doctrine of Space and Time, his refutation of Idealism, and his discussion of the Antinomies of the Pure Reason, are almost without a parallel in the History of Philosophy. W. H. STANLEY MONCK.

Trinity College, Jan. 22.

In answer to my invitation, Mr. Lewes now 'freely admits that Kant nowhere speaks of Space and Time as "Forms of Thought,"' but still contends that 'Kant would not have disclaimed such language, as misrepresenting his meaning.' As well might he argue that although Euclid never uses the word *epipedon* (our English word *plane* or *plain*), to signify a curved surface (*ἐπίφανεια*), he would not have remonstrated against the use of the term *cylindrical epipedon* or conical *epipedon*, to denote the surface of a cylinder or cone, in a professed exposition or criticism of his Elements of Geometry, because in common life we speak of rough or undulating plains, or because a plane admits of being bent into the shape of a cylindrical or conical surface. I think the ladies who are getting up their Planes and Solids at St. George's Hall would be of a different opinion from Mr. Lewes in this matter, and with good reason on their side.

Mr. Lewes, reiterating a statement contained in his previous letter, goes out of his way to affirm that he 'uniformly speaks of Space and Time as forms of Intuition in his pages of exposition' of Kant's doctrine in his 'History of Philosophy.' Were the fact so, it would not in any material degree excuse the inaccuracy of subsequently styling them 'Forms of Thought;' and, moreover, the real point at issue is not Mr. Lewes's general accuracy or inaccuracy, but whether a mode of speech which he, along with others, employs, is right in itself and ought to be persisted in.

However, as Mr. Lewes has thought fit to put in a sort of plea in mitigation of former wrong-doing, I have taken the trouble of looking through his *exposition* and *criticism* of Kant in his History (ed. 1867) and in no single instance have I come upon the phrase *forms of intuition* applied to Space and Time, either in the one or the other; although he states he has *uniformly spoken of them* as such in the former. I have marked the word *intuitions* as occurring once, and *forms of sensibility* several times, but *forms of intuition* never. If *form of sensibility* is as good to use as *form of intuition*, *form of understanding* ought to be as good as *form of thought*; but Mr. Lewes owns that the former is indefensible, whilst he avers that the latter is correct. If Mr. Lewes has ever called Space and Time *forms of intuition* in the History, it will be easy for him to set me right by quoting the passage where the phrase occurs, although that circumstance would not in any degree better his own position, and still less excuse the assertion of his *uniform* use of the term.

If Mr. Lewes cannot quote correctly from his own writings, it will surprise nobody that he misquotes the language of an opponent. He repeats, 'Intuition without thought is mere sensuous impression,' and adds, 'Mr. Sylvester demurs to this.' My words are (*Nature*, Jan. 13, 1870): 'To such a misuse of the word energy it would be little to the point to urge that *force without energy is mere potential tendency*. It is just as little to the point in the matter at issue for Mr. Lewes to inform the readers of *Nature* that *intuition without thought is mere sensuous impression*.' So that, according to Mr. Lewes, to say that a proposition is *little to the point* is *demurring to its truth*.

I should not hesitate to say if some amiable youth wished to entertain his partner in a quadrille with agreeable conversation, that it would be *little to the point*, according to the German proverb, to regale her with such information as how

'Long are the days of summer-tide,
And tall the towers of Strasburg's fane,'

but should be surprised to have it imputed to me on that account that I demurred to the proposition of the length of the days in summer, or the height of Strasburg's towers.

In another passage, Mr. Lewes gives me credit for 'saying correctly that Intuition and Thought are not convertible terms'— a platitude I never dreamed of giving utterance to; but that I am 'incorrect in assuming that they differ as potential and actual'—words which, or the like of which, in any sort or sense, never flowed from my pen. Surely this is not fair controversy, to misquote the words and allegations of an opponent. It seems to me too much like fighting with poisoned weapons. I decline to continue the contest on such terms; and, passing over Mr. Lewes's very odd statement about *species* and *genus* with reference to Intuition and Thought, shall conclude with expressing my surprise at his and Mr. G. C. Robertson's confident assumption that Kant uses in the title of his book *pure reason* in a far wider sense than in the body of his work, simply because to arrive at the Pure Reason he has to *go through* the Critick of the Sensibility and of the Understanding. If in a history of the Reign of Queen Victoria the author should find it expedient to go back to the times of the Norman and Saxon conquests, would it be right to infer therefrom that he used in his title-page the name Victoria in a generalised sense, to include not only her most Gracious Majesty, but also the Tanner's daughter and Princess Rowena?

Perhaps by this time many of the Naturalistic readers of the journal who regard the human intelligence as forming no part of the scheme of Nature, wish Space at the bottom of the sea; but the more the subject is canvassed, and the greater the number of English authorities brought forward to back up Mr. Lewes in wresting the words of Kant from their proper scientific signification, the higher meed of praise seems to me to accrue to Dr. Ingleby for stemming the tide of depravation, and banishing, as I feel confident this discussion will have the effect of doing, from the realm of English would-be philosophy, such a loose and incautious way of talking as that of giving to Space and Time the designation which the Master has appropriated to the categories of his system, and to them alone.   J. J. SYLVESTER.

P.S.—I should be doing injustice to the very sincere sentiments of respect I entertain for Mr. Lewes's varied and brilliant attainments (which constitute him a kind of link between the material and spiritual sides of Nature), and of gratitude for the pleasure the perusal of his 'History of Philosophy' has afforded me, were I to part company with him without disclaiming all acrimony of feeling, if perchance any too strident tones should have seemed to mingle with my enforced reply. In naming him in the original offending footnote (the fountain of these tears), my purpose was simply to emphasise the necessity of protesting against what seemed to me an unsound form of words, *apropos* of Kant, which went on receiving countenance from such and so eminent writers as himself and the others named; and I should be false to my own instincts did I not at heart admire the courageous spirit with which, almost unaided and alone (like a good, I meant to say valiant knight of old), he has done his best to defend his position and maintain his ground against all opposers.

J. J. S.

I am quite willing to leave the readers of *Nature* and the students of Kant to decide on the propriety, in English philosophical discourse, of calling Space and Time 'forms of Thought,' the more so as Sir W. Hamilton—a great stickler for philosophic precision—uses the term in that sense and would have been surprised to hear that he had misrepresented Kant in so doing. My opponents persist in limiting the term Thought to the restricted meaning given to it in Kant's terminology, which, in English, is restricting it to Conception or Judgment: on this ground they might deny that Imagination or Recollection could be properly spoken of as Thought. Throughout I have accepted Thought as equivalent to mental activity in general and the 'forms of Thought' as the conditions of such activity. The 'forms of Thought' are the forms which the thinking principle (Kant's *pure* Reason) brings with it, antecedent to all experience. The thinking principle acts through three distinct faculties: Sensibility (Intuition), Understanding (Conception), and Reason (Ratiocination): to suppose Thought absent from Intuition, is to reduce Intuition to mere sensuous impression. Therefore, whatever is a form of Intuition must be a form of Thought.

The following passage from Mr. Mahaffy's valuable translation of Kuno Fischer's work on Kant, may here be useful: 'Sensibility and understanding are cognitive faculties differing not in degree but in kind, and form the *two original faculties of the human mind*' .... The general problem of a Critick of the Reason ' is subdivided into two particular objects, as human Reason is into two particular faculties of knowledge. The first object is the investigation of the sensibility; the second, that of the understanding. The first question is, How is rational knowledge possible through sensibility? The second question, How is the same knowledge possible through the understanding?' (pp. 4, 5.)

Those who maintain that it is improper to speak of Space and Time as forms of Thought, must either maintain that Kant held Sensibility *not* to be a faculty of the Mind (thinking principle); or that the term Thought is *not*, in English discourse, a correct expression for the activity of the thinking principle. I believe that the student will agree with me in saying that, although Kant restricted the term Thought to what we call Conception or Judgment, he understood by the activity of the mental faculties (Pure Reason) what we understand by Thought.

It is not, however, to continue this discussion that I again trespass on your space; but to reply to the personal part of Mr. Sylvester's letter. He charges me with misquoting myself and with misquoting him. I said that, in my exposition, Space and Time were uniformly spoken of as forms of Intuition and I say so still. Mr. Sylvester has taken the trouble of reading that exposition without taking the trouble of understanding it; he declares that he 'has marked the word intuition as occurring once and forms of sensibility several times; but forms of intuition never.' His *carefulness* may be estimated by the fact that the word intuition occurs *four* times on the two pages: his *comprehension* by the fact that it is perfectly indifferent whether Sensibility or Intuition be the term employed, since sensibility is the faculty and Intuition the action of that faculty. Mr. Sylvester, not understanding this, says, 'If form of sensibility is as good to use as form of intuition, form of understanding ought to be as good as form of thought; but Mr. Lewes owns that the former is indefensible, whilst he avers that the latter is correct.' Considering that this passage occurs in a letter which charges me with unfair misquotation, it is curious. So far from owning that the former is 'indefensible,' it is what I declare to be true; and, with regard to the latter, though I do think a form of Understanding is a form of Thought, my statement was altogether away from it, namely, that Space and Time as forms of Sensibility, would be incorrectly spoken of as forms of the Understanding.

With regard to the alleged misquotation of his own words, which he characterises as unfair and as 'too much like fighting with poisoned weapons,' it was a charge which both astonished and pained me. There are few things for which I have a bitterer contempt than taking such unfair advantages of an adversary. I beg to apologise to Professor Sylvester for any misrepresentation which, unintentionally, I may have been guilty of. But, in accepting his denial of the construction I placed upon his language, I must still say that, after re-reading his letter I am at a loss to see what other construction it admits of, that has any bearing on the dispute, and that he has not expressed his meaning with sufficient clearness. Intuition and Thought are there compared with Force and Energy as terms 'not convertible'; Force is detached from Energy as potential from actual, and Intuition without Thought is made to hold an analogous position. Here is the passage; let the reader judge:—

'Can Mr. Lewes point to any passage in Kant where Space and Time are designated *forms of thought*? I shall indeed be surprised if he can do so—as much surprised as if Mr. Todhunter or Mr. Routh in their Mechanical Treatises were to treat *energy* and *force* as convertible terms. To such a misuse of the word energy it would be little to the point to urge that *force without energy is a mere potential tendency*. It is just as little to the point, in the matter at issue, for Mr. Lewes to inform the readers of *Nature* that *intuition without thought is mere sensuous impression*.'

Is it to use 'poisoned weapons' to interpret this as assuming that Intuition and Thought differ as potential and actual? I repeat that, since Mr. Sylvester disclaims the interpretation, my only course is to apologise for it; but, after his own misinterpretations of me, he will not, I hope, persist in attributing mine to a desire to take an unfair advantage. If I make no reply to the other points raised in the various letters it is in order not to prolong the discussion.

GEORGE HENRY LEWES.

I DO not know whether Mr. Sylvester and Dr. Ingleby will be satisfied with Mr. Lewes' letter in yours of the 27th. I am not, and I think, in defending his former mistake, Mr. Lewes has fallen into additional errors.

It is undoubtedly fair to translate an author into your own language before criticising him, provided you found no criticism on the language that you have put into his mouth. But this I think Mr. Lewes has done. He accuses Kant of inconsistency in speaking of pure *à priori* cognitions, when, on his own system, pure thought only supplies one element to these cognitions, the other being derived from sense or intuition. Now (not to insist here that Kant constantly uses the term cognition in a wider sense than that which Mr. Lewes insists on fastening upon him), this criticism is evidently invalidated by the simple remark that Kant admits pure intuitions as well as pure concepts, and explains the nature of mathematics, as a system of *à priori* cognitions, by the fact that its object-matter consists of nothing but pure intuitions.

Mr. Lewes now informs us that Kant's Intuition and Thought 'differ as species and genus.' According to Kant they differ in kind; and Leibnitz was as wrong in making sensibility a species of thought as Locke was in making Thought a species of sensibility. Space and Time, Mr. Lewes adds, are forms of 'mental activity' and, therefore, are properly termed 'forms of Thought,' in the meaning of the latter term which is usually current in this country. If they were forms of mental activity they would be forms of Thought, according to Kant, likewise; for the criterion by which Kant distinguishes between Intuition and Thought (under which term he includes both the understanding proper and the reason proper) is that, in the former, the mind is passive (receptive) while, in the latter, it is spontaneously active; and it is precisely on this ground—the passive reception of them by the mind—that he refers Space and Time to Sensibility rather than Thought. This is repeatedly brought out in the Transcendental Deduction of the Categories. See in particular Sections 11 (Meiklejohn, p. 80) and 18 (Meiklejohn, p. 90).

I think if Mr. Lewes will turn to the preface to the first edition of the 'Critick,' he will see that the transcendental logic only (and perhaps I might limit it to the transcendental dialectic) grapples *directly* with the problem indicated by the title of the book. The Aesthetic is a preliminary inquiry, which proves afterwards of great use; but is not to be considered as a Critick of Pure Reason in this particular department. His using the term 'concept' of space, is certainly confusing; but its explanation, I think, is to be found in a passage in the 'Transcendental Exposition' of this 'concept' (Meiklejohn, p. 25), where he says, 'It must be *originally* intuition, for from a *mere* conception no propositions can be deducted which go out beyond the conception, and this happens in geometry.' In the preceding page he similarly qualifies his statement that Space is an intuition. 'No conception *as such*,' he says, 'can be so conceived as if it contained, within itself, an infinite multitude of representations.' We may now have a concept as well as an intuition of Space and Time; but the intuition was the original form of the idea, and it is to the intuition that we must always have recourse in mathematics when we wish to discover a new truth.

I think, if Mr. Lewes will again read over the Transcendental Aesthetic and the parts of the Transcendental Analytic which are closely related to it, he will see that Kant never designates the *original* representations of space and time 'concepts,' or refers their origin to 'pure reason.' W. H. STANLEY MONCK.

Trinity College, Dublin. Jan. 29.

[This correspondence must now cease.—ED.]

In order that the reader may judge of the correctness of the assertions made by Mr. Lewes in his concluding letter, and his general fairness in controversy, I request attention to the annexed *catena* of passages drawn from the above correspondence.*

No. 1. The AUTHOR.

'It is very common not to say universal with English writers even such authorised' (I meant to say authoritative) 'ones as Whewell, Lewes or Herbert Spencer to refer to Kant's doctrine as affirming space to be "a form of thought," or "of the understanding." This is putting into Kant's mouth words which he would have been the first to disclaim.'

No. 2. Mr. G. H. LEWES.

(α) 'Kant assuredly did teach as Professor Sylvester says, and as I HAVE REPEATEDLY STATED, THAT SPACE IS A FORM OF INTUITION.'

(β) 'Every student of Kant knows that intuition without thought is mere sensuous impression.'

(γ) 'While therefore anyone who spoke of space as "A FORM OF THE UNDERSTANDING" WOULD CERTAINLY USE LANGUAGE WHICH KANT WOULD HAVE DISCLAIMED, Kant himself would have been surprised to hear that space was not held by him as a form of thought.'

[(α) In no one single instance in his fifty pages of exposition and criticism has Mr. Lewes ever once stated that *Space is a Form of Intuition.*]

No. 3. The AUTHOR.

'Can Mr. Lewes point to any passage in Kant where Space and Time are designated *forms of thought*. I shall indeed be

* The words in SMALL CAPITALS are in ordinary print in the original passages.

much surprised if he can do so—as much surprised as if Mr. Todhunter or Mr. Routh in their mechanical treatises were to treat *energy* and *force* as convertible terms. To such a misuse of the word energy it would be as little to the point to urge that *force without energy is mere potential tendency*. It is just as LITTLE TO THE POINT in the matter at issue for Mr. Lewes to inform the readers of *Nature* that *intuition without thought is mere potential tendency*.'

No. 4. Mr. G. H. Lewes.

'In the pages of exposition *I uniformly speak of Space and Time as forms of intuition*; no language can be plainer.' [In no one single instance does Mr. Lewes so speak of Space or Time.]

(α) 'Mr. Sylvester correctly says that intuition and thought are not convertible terms. (β) But he is incorrect in affirming that they differ as potential and actual.'

[These are words put into my mouth by Mr. Lewes, which I disclaim as Kant would have disclaimed the words put into his. I nowhere have stated the truism (α). I nowhere have affirmed the absurdity (β).]

No. 5. Mr. G. Croom Robertson.

'If indeed any of them ever speaks of space as a "form of the understanding," which was part of the original charge, the case is very different, Kant being so careful with his *Verstand*. But Mr. Lewes at least would never be caught speaking thus.'

No. 6. The Author.

'(α) If form of sensibility is as good to use as form of intuition, form of understanding ought to be as good to use as form of thought (β), but Mr. Lewes owns that the former is indefensible whilst he avers that the latter is correct.'

[In proof of (β) above see (γ) of No. 2. (α) above evidently implies the proportion :—

  sensibility : Intuition :: understanding : thought.

The first and third terms representing faculties, the second and fourth the actions of those faculties respectively.]

No. 7. Mr. G. H. Lewes.

'His [the author's] *carefulness* may be estimated by the (α) fact that the word intuition occurs four times on THE TWO PAGES; his *comprehension* by the fact that it is perfectly indifferent whether Sensibility or Intuition be the term employed, since Sensibility is the faculty and Intuition the action of that faculty. (β) Mr. Sylvester not understanding this, says, "if form of sensibility is as good to use as form of intuition, form of understanding ought to be as good as form of thought; but Mr. Lewes owns that the former is indefensible whilst he avers that the latter is correct." (γ) So far from averring that the former (form of understanding) is "indefensible," it is what I declare to be true.'

(δ) 'I said that in my exposition Space and Time were uniformly spoken of as forms of intuition, and I say so still.'

As regards (α) what does Mr. Lewes mean by the use of the definite article THE? The whole question was about the use of the phrase *forms of intuition*; it was a mere work of surplusage in me to count the number of times that the word *intuition* unsupported occurs; but I did wade through the whole of the criticism and exposition, covering between them 50 pages, viz. 35 of exposition (439–474), 15 of criticism (474–489). I can only account for my inadvertence in this quite immaterial point by supposing that a clerical or typographical error (no one who knows my handwriting would wonder at this) has crept in, and that I probably meant to say, as I ought to have said, not 'once' but 'more than once' or 'often.'

(β) How, in the face of the proportion so plainly indicated in No. 6, Mr. Lewes could have the hardihood to make such an assertion is to me incomprehensible.

(γ) This statement is in direct contradiction to what Mr. Lewes has stated in his first letter see No. 2 (γ).

(δ) This assertion is simply untrue. Mr. Lowes has *in no one single instance in his exposition*, or his criticism, 3rd edition, 1867, spoken of 'Space and Time as forms of Intuition.' As Mr. Lewes and myself are here at direct variance on a matter of fact, I undertake to pay £50 to anyone who will discover a single instance where the phrase 'form of Intuition' occurs in Mr.

Lewes' article on Kant, chaps. i., ii., iii., p. 436–489, 3rd edition, 1867.

So much, and more than I could have wished, in the way of settling the personal issue raised by Mr. Lewes. The original and only worthy part of the controversy is one of much greater consequence than the proof or disproof of Mr. Lewes' trustworthiness and self-consistency.

The question to be decided was whether a form of language conveying a completely erroneous view of the fundamental principles of Kant's philosophy was to be adhered to by English writers on the ground of prescription and authority. I think that that question, thanks to Dr. Ingleby's intrepidity and Mr. Lewes' persistency, has now been settled for once and for ever.

In looking over Mr. Lewes's article on Kant for the third or fourth time, to satisfy myself (in the face of his positive and reiterated asseverations to the contrary) that he had not in any one single instance used the phrase 'form of intuition,' I came upon the following passage in a footnote:—

'Mr. Spencer seems to me less happy in his objection that "if space and time are forms of thought, they can never be thought of; since it is impossible for anything to be at once the *form* of thought and the *matter* of thought." '—*First Principles*, p. 49.

Such an observation proceeding from so able a writer as Mr. Herbert Spencer, is a very instructive instance of the serious practical mischief arising from the habit (so obstinately defended by Mr. Lewes) of ascribing to

Kant the statement of Space and Time being forms of Thought. It is clear that if Mr. Spencer had been made aware of the broad line of demarcation in Kant's system between Intuition, the action or product of Sensibility, and Thought the action or product of the Understanding (the two belonging, according to Kant, to entirely different provinces of the mind), he would have seen that his supposed refutation proceeded on a mere misapprehension of Kant's actual utterance and doctrine on the subject. If Mr. Spencer will restore to Kant the words really used by him, the sentence will run thus: 'if space and time are forms of intuition, they can never be thought of; since it is impossible for anything to be at once the *form* of thought and the *matter* of thought;' and his epigram (for Mr. Spencer must have meant it rather as an epigram than as a serious argument) loses all its point. Was it likely à *priori* that Kant (*the* Kant) should have laid himself open to such a *scholar's-mate* at the very outset of his system?

ATHENÆUM CLUB,
   July, 1870.

[JULY 1870.]

GENERAL LIST OF WORKS

PUBLISHED BY

Messrs. LONGMANS, GREEN, AND CO.

PATERNOSTER ROW, LONDON.

History, Politics, Historical Memoirs, &c.

The **HISTORY of ENGLAND** from the Fall of Wolsey to the Defeat of the Spanish Armada. By JAMES ANTHONY FROUDE, M.A. late Fellow of Exeter College, Oxford.
 LIBRARY EDITION, 12 VOLS. 8vo. price £8 18s.
 CABINET EDITION, now appearing, in 12 vols. crown 8vo. price 6s. each.

The **HISTORY of ENGLAND** from the Accession of James II. By Lord MACAULAY.
  LIBRARY EDITION, 5 vols. 8vo. £4.
  CABINET EDITION, 8 vols. post 8vo. 48s.
  PEOPLE'S EDITION, 4 vols. crown 8vo. 16s.

LORD MACAULAY'S WORKS. Complete and Uniform Library Edition. Edited by his Sister, Lady TREVELYAN. 8 vols. 8vo. with Portrait, price £5 5s. cloth, or £8 8s. bound in tree-calf by Rivière.

An **ESSAY** on the **HISTORY of the ENGLISH GOVERNMENT** and Constitution, from the Reign of Henry VII. to the Present Time. By JOHN EARL RUSSELL. Fourth Edition, revised. Crown 8vo. 6s.

SELECTIONS from SPEECHES of EARL RUSSELL, 1817 to 1841, and from Despatches, 1859 to 1865; with Introductions. 2 vols. 8vo. 28s.

VARIETIES of VICE-REGAL LIFE. By Sir WILLIAM DENISON, K.C.B. late Governor-General of the Australian Colonies, and Governor of Madras. With Two Maps. 2 vols. 8vo. 28s.

On **PARLIAMENTARY GOVERNMENT** in **ENGLAND**: Its Origin, Development, and Practical Operation. By ALPHEUS TODD, Librarian of the Legislative Assembly of Canada. 2 vols. 8vo. price £1 17s.

LAND SYSTEMS and INDUSTRIAL ECONOMY of IRELAND, ENGLAND, and CONTINENTAL COUNTRIES. By T. E. CLIFFE LESLIE, LL.B. of Lincoln's Inn, Barrister-at-Law. 8vo. 12s.

A **HISTORICAL ACCOUNT of the NEUTRALITY of GREAT BRITAIN DURING the AMERICAN CIVIL WAR.** By MOUNTAGUE BERNARD, M.A. Chichele Professor of International Law and Diplomacy in the University of Oxford. Royal 8vo. 16s.

A

The HISTORY of ENGLAND during the Reign of George the Third. By the Right Hon. W. N. Massey. Cabinet Edition. 4 vols. post 8vo. 24s.

The CONSTITUTIONAL HISTORY of ENGLAND, since the Accession of George III. 1760—1860. By Sir Thomas Erskine May, C.B. Second Edition. 2 vols. 8vo. 33s.

HISTORICAL STUDIES. By Herman Merivale, M.A. 8vo. 12s. 6d.

The OXFORD REFORMERS of 1498—John Colet, Erasmus, and Thomas More; being a History of their Fellow-work. By Frederic Seebohm. Second Edition, enlarged. 8vo. 14s.

A HISTORY of WALES, derived from Authentic Sources. By Jane Williams, Ysgafell, Author of a Memoir of the Rev. Thomas Price, and Editor of his Literary Remains. 8vo. 14s.

LECTURES on the HISTORY of ENGLAND, from the earliest Times to the Death of King Edward II. By William Longman. With Maps and Illustrations. 8vo. 15s.

The HISTORY of the LIFE and TIMES of EDWARD the THIRD. By William Longman. With 9 Maps, 8 Plates, and 16 Woodcuts. 2 vols. 8vo. 28s.

HISTORY of the NORMAN KINGS of ENGLAND, from a New Collation of the Contemporary Chronicles. By Thomas Cobbe, Barrister, of the Inner Temple. 8vo. price 16s.

WATERLOO LECTURES: a Study of the Campaign of 1815. By Colonel Charles C. Chesney, R.E. late Professor of Military Art and History in the Staff College. New Edition. 8vo. with Map, 10s. 6d.

DEMOCRACY in AMERICA. By Alexis De Tocqueville. Translated by Henry Reeve. 2 vols. 8vo. 21s.

HISTORY of the REFORMATION in EUROPE in the Time of Calvin. By J. H. Merle D'Aubigné, D.D. Vols. I. and II. 8vo. 28s. Vol. III. 18s. Vol. IV. 16s. Vol. V. price 16s.

HISTORY of FRANCE, from Clovis and Charlemagne to the Accession of Napoléon III. By Eyre Evans Crowe. 5 vols. 8vo. £4 13s.

CHAPTERS from FRENCH HISTORY; St. Louis, Joan of Arc, Henri IV. with Sketches of the Intermediate Periods. By J. H. Gurney, M.A. late Rector of St. Mary's, Marylebone. New Edition. Fcp. 8vo. 6s. 6d.

MEMOIR of POPE SIXTUS the FIFTH. By Baron Hubner. Translated from the Original in French, with the Author's sanction by Hubert E. H. Jerningham. 2 vols. 8vo. [In October.

IGNATIUS LOYOLA and the EARLY JESUITS. By Stewart Rose. 8vo. with Portrait, price 16s.

The HISTORY of GREECE. By C. Thirlwall, D.D. Lord Bishop of St. David's. 8 vols. fcp. 8vo. price 28s.

GREEK HISTORY from Themistocles to Alexander, in a Series of Lives from Plutarch. Revised and arranged by A. H. Clough. Fcp. with 44 Woodcuts, 6s.

CRITICAL HISTORY of the LANGUAGE and LITERATURE of Ancient Greece. By William Mure, of Caldwell. 5 vols. 8vo. £3 9s.

The TALE of the GREAT PERSIAN WAR, from the Histories of Herodotus. By George W. Cox, M.A. New Edition. Fcp. 3s. 6d.

HISTORY of the LITERATURE of ANCIENT GREECE. By Professor K. O. MÜLLER. Translated by the Right Hon. Sir GEORGE CORNEWALL LEWIS, Bart. and by J. W. DONALDSON, D.D. 3 vols. 8vo. 21s.

HISTORY of the CITY of ROME from its Foundation to the Sixteenth Century of the Christian Era. By THOMAS H. DYER, LL.D. 8vo. with 2 Maps, 15s.

ROMAN HISTORY. By WILHELM IHNE. Translated and revised by the Author. VOLS. I. and II. 8vo. The First and Second Volumes of this work will be published together in the present season; and the whole work will be completed in Three or at most Four Volumes.

HISTORY of the ROMANS under the EMPIRE. By the Very Rev. C. MERIVALE, D.C.L. Dean of Ely. 8 vols. post 8vo. 48s.

The FALL of the ROMAN REPUBLIC; a Short History of the Last Century of the Commonwealth. By the same Author. 12mo. 7s. 6d.

The STUDENT'S MANUAL of the HISTORY of INDIA, from the Earliest Period to the Present. By Colonel MEADOWS TAYLOR, M.R.A.S. M.R.I.A. Author of 'The Confessions of a Thug.' Crown 8vo. [*In the press.*

The HISTORY of INDIA, from the Earliest Period to the close of Lord Dalhousie's Administration. By JOHN CLARK MARSHMAN. 3 vols. crown 8vo. 22s. 6d.

INDIAN POLITY: a View of the System of Administration in India. By Lieutenant-Colonel GEORGE CHESNEY, Fellow of the University of Calcutta. New Edition. [*Nearly ready.*

HOME POLITICS; being a consideration of the Causes of the Growth of Trade in relation to Labour, Pauperism, and Emigration. By DANIEL GRANT. 8vo. 7s.

REALITIES of IRISH LIFE. By W. STEUART TRENCH, Land Agent in Ireland to the Marquess of Lansdowne, the Marquess of Bath, and Lord Digby. New and Cheaper Cabinet Edition (being the Fifth). Crown 8vo. price 6s.

The STUDENT'S MANUAL of the HISTORY of IRELAND. By MARY F. CUSACK, Authoress of the 'Illustrated of Ireland, from the Earliest Period to the Year of Catholic Emancipation.' Crown 8vo. price 6s.

CRITICAL and HISTORICAL ESSAYS contributed to the *Edinburgh Review*. By the Right Hon. LORD MACAULAY.
    CABINET EDITION, 4 vols. post 8vo. 24s.
    LIBRARY EDITION, 3 vols. 8vo. 36s.
    PEOPLE'S EDITION, 2 vols. crown 8vo. 8s.
    STUDENT'S EDITION, in One Volume, crown 8vo. 6s.

HISTORY of EUROPEAN MORALS, from Augustus to Charlemagne. By W. E. H. LECKY, M.A. Second Edition. 2 vols. 8vo. price 28s.

HISTORY of the RISE and INFLUENCE of the SPIRIT of RATIONALISM in EUROPE. By W. E. H. LECKY, M.A. Cabinet Edition, being the Fourth. 2 vols. crown 8vo. price 16s.

GOD in HISTORY; or, the Progress of Man's Faith in the Moral Order of the World. By the late Baron BUNSEN. Translated from the German by SUSANNA WINKWORTH; with a Preface by Dean STANLEY. In Three Volumes, 8vo. price 42s.

The **HISTORY** of **PHILOSOPHY**, from Thales to Comte. By GEORGE HENRY LEWES. Third Edition. 2 vols. 8vo. 30s.

The **MYTHOLOGY** of the **ARYAN NATIONS**. By GEORGE W. COX, M.A. late Scholar of Trinity College, Oxford, Joint-Editor with the late Professor Brande, of the Fourth Edition of 'The Dictionary of Science, Literature, and Art,' Author of 'Tales of Ancient Greece,' &c. 2 vols. 8vo. 28s.

EGYPT'S PLACE in **UNIVERSAL HISTORY**; an Historical Investigation. By Baron BUNSEN, D.C.L. Translated by C. H. COTTRELL, M.A. With Additions by S. BIRCH, LL.D. 5 vols. 8vo. price £8 14s. 6d.

HISTORY of **CIVILISATION** in England and France, Spain and Scotland. By HENRY THOMAS BUCKLE. New Edition of the entire Work, with a complete INDEX. 3 vols. crown 8vo. 24s.

HISTORY of the **CHRISTIAN CHURCH**, from the Ascension of Christ to the Conversion of Constantine. By E. BURTON, D.D. late Prof. of Divinity in the Univ. of Oxford. Eighth Edition. Fcp. 3s. 6d.

SKETCH of the **HISTORY** of the **CHURCH** of **ENGLAND** to the Revolution of 1688. By the Right Rev. T. V. SHORT, D.D. Lord Bishop of St. Asaph. Eighth Edition. Crown 8vo. 7s. 6d.

HISTORY of the **EARLY CHURCH**, from the First Preaching of the Gospel to the Council of Nicaea, A.D. 325. By ELIZABETH M. SEWELL, Author of 'Amy Herbert.' New Edition, with Questions. Fcp. 4s. 6d.

The **ENGLISH REFORMATION**. By F. C. MASSINGBERD, M.A. Chancellor of Lincoln and Rector of South Ormsby. Fourth Edition, revised. Fcp. 8vo. 7s. 6d.

MAUNDER'S HISTORICAL TREASURY; comprising a General Introductory Outline of Universal History, and a series of Separate Histories. Latest Edition, revised and brought down to the Present Time by the Rev. GEORGE WILLIAM COX, M.A. Fcp. 6s. cloth, or 9s. 6d. calf.

WOODWARD'S HISTORICAL and **CHRONOLOGICAL ENCYCLOPÆDIA**.—The copious 'Encyclopædia of Chronology and History,' projected and left unfinished by the late B. B. WOODWARD, H.A. F.S.A. Librarian to the Queen at Windsor, is in an advanced state of preparation, and will be completed by Mr. W. L. R. CATES, Editor of the *Dictionary of General Biography*, the friend, and for ten years the collaborateur, of Mr. WOODWARD.

Biographical Works.

The **LIFE** and **LETTERS** of **FARADAY**. By Dr. BENCE JONES, Secretary of the Royal Institution. Second Edition, thoroughly revised. 2 vols. 8vo. with Portrait, and Eight Engravings on Wood, price 28s.

FARADAY as a **DISCOVERER**. By JOHN TYNDALL, LL.D. F.R.S. Professor of Natural Philosophy in the Royal Institution. New and Cheaper Edition, with Two Portraits. Fcp. 8vo. 3s. 6d.

The **LIFE** and **LETTERS** of the **Rev. SYDNEY SMITH**. Edited by his Daughter, Lady HOLLAND, and Mrs. AUSTIN. New Edition, complete in One Volume. Crown 8vo. price 6s.

A **MEMOIR** of **GEORGE EDWARD LYNCH COTTON**, D.D. late Lord Bishop of Calcutta; with Selections from his Journals and Letters. Edited by Mrs. COTTON. [*In preparation.*

The **LIFE** of **OLIVER CROMWELL**, to the Death of Charles I. By J. R. ANDREWS, Barrister-at-Law. 8vo. 14s.

DICTIONARY of **GENERAL BIOGRAPHY**; containing Concise Memoirs and Notices of the most Eminent Persons of all Countries, from the Earliest Ages to the Present Time. Edited by W. L. R. CATES. 8vo. 21s.

LIVES of the **TUDOR PRINCESSES**, including Lady Jane Grey and her Sisters. By AGNES STRICKLAND, Author of 'Lives of the Queens of England.' Post 8vo. with Portrait, &c. 12s. 6d.

LIVES of the **QUEENS** of **ENGLAND**. By AGNES STRICKLAND. Library Edition, newly revised; with Portraits of every Queen, Autographs, and Vignettes. 8 vols. post 8vo. 7s. 6d. each.

MEMOIRS of **BARON BUNSEN**. Drawn chiefly from Family Papers by his Widow, FRANCES Baroness BUNSEN. Second Edition, abridged; with 2 Portraits and 4 Woodcuts. 2 vols. post 8vo. 21s.

The **LETTERS** of the **Right Hon. Sir GEORGE CORNEWALL LEWIS**, Bart. to various Friends. Edited by his Brother, the Rev. Canon Sir G. F. LEWIS, Bart. 8vo. with Portrait, price 14s.

LIFE of the **DUKE** of **WELLINGTON**. By the Rev. G. R. GLEIG, M.A. Popular Edition, carefully revised; with copious Additions. Crown 8vo. with Portrait, 5s.

HISTORY of **MY RELIGIOUS OPINIONS**. By J. H. NEWMAN, D.D. Being the Substance of Apologia pro Vita Suâ. Post 8vo. 6s.

FATHER MATHEW: a Biography. By JOHN FRANCIS MAGUIRE, M.P. for Cork. Popular Edition, with Portrait. Crown 8vo. 3s. 6d.

FELIX MENDELSSOHN'S LETTERS from *Italy and Switzerland*, and *Letters from 1833 to 1847*, translated by Lady WALLACE. New Edition, with Portrait. 2 vols. crown 8vo. 5s. each.

MEMOIRS of **SIR HENRY HAVELOCK, K.C.B.** By JOHN CLARK MARSHMAN. Cabinet Edition, with Portrait. Crown 8vo. price 3s. 6d.

CAPTAIN COOK'S LIFE, VOYAGES, and DISCOVERIES. 18mo. Woodcuts, 2s. 6d.

VICISSITUDES of **FAMILIES**. By Sir J. BERNARD BURKE, C.B. Ulster King of Arms. New Edition, remodelled and enlarged. 2 vols. crown 8vo. 21s.

THE EARLS of **GRANARD**: a Memoir of the Noble Family of Forbes. Written by Admiral the Hon. JOHN FORBES, and edited by GEORGE ARTHUR HASTINGS, present Earl of Granard, K.P. 8vo. 10s.

ESSAYS in **ECCLESIASTICAL BIOGRAPHY**. By the Right Hon. Sir J. STEPHEN, LL.D. Cabinet Edition, being the Fifth. Crown 8vo. 7s. 6d.

MAUNDER'S BIOGRAPHICAL TREASURY. Thirteenth Edition, reconstructed, thoroughly revised, and in great part rewritten; with about 1,000 additional Memoirs and Notices, by W. L. R. CATES. Fcp. 6s.

LETTERS and **LIFE** of **FRANCIS BACON**, including all his Occasional Works. Collected and edited, with a Commentary, by J. SPEDDING, Trin. Coll. Cantab. VOLS. I. and II. 8vo. 24s. VOLS. III. and IV. 24s. VOL. V. price 12s.

Criticism, Philosophy, Polity, &c.

The **INSTITUTES of JUSTINIAN**; with English Introduction, Translation, and Notes. By T. C. SANDARS, M.A. Barrister, late Fellow of Oriel Coll. Oxon. New Edition. 8vo. 15s.

SOCRATES and the SOCRATIC SCHOOLS. Translated from the German of Dr. E. ZELLER, with the Author's approval, by the Rev. OSWALD J. REICHEL, B.C.L. and M.A. Crown 8vo. 8s. 6d.

The **STOICS, EPICUREANS, and SCEPTICS.** Translated from the German of Dr. E. ZELLER, with the Author's approval, by OSWALD J. REICHEL, B.C.L. and M.A. Crown 8vo. price 14s.

The **ETHICS of ARISTOTLE**, Illustrated with Essays and Notes. By Sir A. GRANT, Bart. M.A. LL.D. Second Edition, revised and completed. 2 vols. 8vo. price 28s.

The **NICOMACHEAN ETHICS of ARISTOTLE** newly translated into English. By R. WILLIAMS, B.A. Fellow and late Lecturer of Merton College, and sometime Student of Christ Church, Oxford. 8vo. 12s.

ELEMENTS of LOGIC. By R. WHATELY, D.D. late Archbishop of Dublin. New Edition. 8vo. 10s. 6d. crown 8vo. 4s. 6d.

Elements of Rhetoric. By the same Author. New Edition. 8vo. 10s. 6d. crown 8vo. 4s. 6d.

English Synonymes. By E. JANE WHATELY. Edited by Archbishop WHATELY. 5th Edition. Fcp. 3s.

BACON'S ESSAYS with ANNOTATIONS. By R. WHATELY, D.D. late Archbishop of Dublin. Sixth Edition. 8vo. 10s. 6d.

LORD BACON'S WORKS, collected and edited by J. SPEDDING, M.A. R. L. ELLIS, M.A. and D. D. HEATH. New and Cheaper Edition. 7 vols. 8vo. price £3 13s. 6d.

ENGLAND and IRELAND. By JOHN STUART MILL. Fifth Edition, 8vo. 1s.

The **SUBJECTION of WOMEN.** By JOHN STUART MILL. New Edition. Post 8vo. 5s.

On **REPRESENTATIVE GOVERNMENT.** By JOHN STUART MILL. Third Edition. 8vo. 9s. Crown 8vo. 2s.

On **LIBERTY.** By JOHN STUART MILL. Fourth Edition. Post 8vo. 7s. 6d. Crown 8vo. 1s. 4d.

Principles of Political Economy. By the same Author. Sixth Edition. 2 vols. 8vo. 30s. Or in 1 vol. crown 8vo. 5s.

A System of Logic, Ratiocinative and Inductive. By the same Author. Seventh Edition. Two vols. 8vo. 25s.

ANALYSIS of Mr. MILL'S SYSTEM of LOGIC. By W. STEBBING, M.A. Fellow of Worcester College, Oxford. New Edition. 12mo. 3s. 6d.

UTILITARIANISM. By JOHN STUART MILL. Third Edition. 8vo. 5s.

DISSERTATIONS and DISCUSSIONS, POLITICAL, PHILOSOPHICAL, and HISTORICAL. By JOHN STUART MILL. Second Edition, revised. 3 vols. 8vo. 36s.

EXAMINATION of Sir W. HAMILTON'S PHILOSOPHY, and of the Principal Philosophical Questions discussed in his Writings. By JOHN STUART MILL. Third Edition. 8vo. 14s.

An OUTLINE of the NECESSARY LAWS of THOUGHT: a Treatise on Pure and Applied Logic. By the Most Rev. WILLIAM, Lord Archbishop of York, D.D. F.R.S. Ninth Thousand. Crown 8vo. 5s. 6d.

The ELEMENTS of POLITICAL ECONOMY. By HENRY DUNNING MACLEOD, M.A. Barrister-at-Law. 8vo. 16s.

A Dictionary of Political Economy; Biographical, Bibliographical, Historical, and Practical. By the same Author. VOL. I. royal 8vo. 30s.

The ELECTION of REPRESENTATIVES, Parliamentary and Municipal; a Treatise. By THOMAS HARE, Barrister-at-Law. Third Edition, with Additions. Crown 8vo. 6s.

SPEECHES of the RIGHT HON. LORD MACAULAY, corrected by Himself. People's Edition, crown 8vo. 3s. 6d.

Lord Macaulay's Speeches on Parliamentary Reform in 1831 and 1832. 16mo. 1s.

INAUGURAL ADDRESS delivered to the University of St. Andrews. By JOHN STUART MILL. 8vo. 5s. People's Edition, crown 8vo. 1s.

A DICTIONARY of the ENGLISH LANGUAGE. By R. G. LATHAM, M.A. M.D. F.R.S. Founded on the Dictionary of Dr. SAMUEL JOHNSON, as edited by the Rev. H. J. TODD, with numerous Emendations and Additions. In Four Volumes, 4to. price £7.

THESAURUS of ENGLISH WORDS and PHRASES, classified and arranged so as to facilitate the Expression of Ideas, and assist in Literary Composition. By P. M. ROGET, M.D. New Edition. Crown 8vo. 10s. 6d.

LECTURES on the SCIENCE of LANGUAGE, delivered at the Royal Institution. By MAX MÜLLER, M.A. Fellow of All Souls College, Oxford. 2 vols. 8vo. price 30s.

CHAPTERS on LANGUAGE. By FREDERIC W. FARRAR, F.R.S. late Fellow of Trin. Coll. Cambridge. Crown 8vo. 8s. 6d.

WORD-GOSSIP; a Series of Familiar Essays on Words and their Peculiarities. By the Rev. W. L. BLACKLEY, M.A. Fcp. 8vo. 5s.

A BOOK ABOUT WORDS. By G. F. GRAHAM, Author of 'English, or the Art of Composition,' &c. Fcp. 8vo. price 3s. 6d.

The DEBATER; a Series of Complete Debates, Outlines of Debates, and Questions for Discussion. By F. ROWTON. Fcp. 6s.

MANUAL of ENGLISH LITERATURE, Historical and Critical. By THOMAS ARNOLD, M.A. Second Edition. Crown 8vo. price 7s. 6d.

SOUTHEY'S DOCTOR, complete in One Volume. Edited by the Rev. J. W. WARTER, B.D. Square crown 8vo. 12s. 6d.

HISTORICAL and CRITICAL COMMENTARY on the OLD TESTAMENT; with a New Translation. By M. M. KALISCH, Ph.D. VOL. I. *Genesis*, 8vo. 18s. or adapted for the General Reader, 12s. VOL. II. *Exodus*, 15s. or adapted for the General Reader, 12s. VOL. III. *Leviticus*, PART I. 15s. or adapted for the General Reader, 8s.

A HEBREW GRAMMAR, with EXERCISES. By M. M. KALISCH, Ph.D. PART I. *Outlines with Exercises*, 8vo. 12s. 6d. KEY, 5s. PART II. *Exceptional Forms and Constructions*, 12s. 6d.

A LATIN-ENGLISH DICTIONARY. By J. T. WHITE, D.D. of Corpus Christi College, and J. E. RIDDLE, M.A. of St. Edmund Hall, Oxford. Third Edition, revised. 2 vols. 4to. pp. 2,128, price 42s. cloth.

White's College Latin-English Dictionary (Intermediate Size), abridged for the use of University Students from the Parent Work (as above). Medium 8vo. pp. 1,048, price 18s. cloth.

White's Junior Student's Complete Latin-English and English-Latin Dictionary. New Edition. Square 12mo. pp. 1,054, price 12s.

Separately { The ENGLISH-LATIN DICTIONARY, price 5s. 6d.
{ The LATIN-ENGLISH DICTIONARY, price 7s. 6d.

An ENGLISH-GREEK LEXICON, containing all the Greek Words used by Writers of good authority. By C. D. YONGE, B.A. New Edition. 4to. 21s.

Mr. YONGE'S NEW LEXICON, English and Greek, abridged from his larger work (as above). Revised Edition. Square 12mo. 8s. 6d.

A GREEK-ENGLISH LEXICON. Compiled by H. G. LIDDELL, D.D. Dean of Christ Church, and R. SCOTT, D.D. Master of Balliol. Sixth Edition. Crown 4to. price 36s.

A Lexicon, Greek and English, abridged from LIDDELL and SCOTT's *Greek-English Lexicon*. Twelfth Edition. Square 12mo. 7s. 6d.

A SANSKRIT-ENGLISH DICTIONARY, the Sanskrit words printed both in the original Devanagari and in Roman Letters. Compiled by T. BENFEY, Prof. in the Univ. of Göttingen. 8vo. 52s. 6d.

WALKER'S PRONOUNCING DICTIONARY of the ENGLISH LANGUAGE. Thoroughly revised Editions, by B. H. SMART. 8vo. 12s. 10mo. 6s.

A PRACTICAL DICTIONARY of the FRENCH and ENGLISH LANGUAGES. By L. CONTANSEAU. Fourteenth Edition. Post 8vo. 10s. 6d.

Contanseau's Pocket Dictionary, French and English, abridged from the above by the Author. New Edition, revised. Square 18mo. 3s. 6d.

NEW PRACTICAL DICTIONARY of the GERMAN LANGUAGE; German-English and English-German. By the Rev. W. L. BLACKLEY, M.A. and Dr. CARL MARTIN FRIEDLÄNDER. Post 8vo. 7s. 6d.

The MASTERY of LANGUAGES; or, the Art of Speaking Foreign Tongues Idiomatically. By THOMAS PRENDERGAST, late of the Civil Service at Madras. Second Edition. 8vo. 6s.

Miscellaneous Works and *Popular Metaphysics.*

The ESSAYS and CONTRIBUTIONS of A. K. H. B., Author of 'The Recreations of a Country Parson.' Uniform Editions:—

Recreations of a Country Parson. By A. K. H. B. FIRST and SECOND SERIES, crown 8vo. 3s. 6d. each.

The Common-place Philosopher in Town and Country. By A. K.
H. B. Crown 8vo. price 3s. 6d.

Leisure Hours in Town; Essays Consolatory, Æsthetical, Moral,
Social, and Domestic. By A. K. H. B. Crown 8vo. 3s. 6d.

The Autumn Holidays of a Country Parson; Essays contributed
to *Fraser's Magazine* and to *Good Words*. By A. K. H. B. Crown 8vo. 3s. 6d.

The Graver Thoughts of a Country Parson. By A. K. H. B. First
and Second Series, crown 8vo. 3s. 6d. each.

Critical Essays of a Country Parson, selected from Essays contributed to *Fraser's Magazine*. By A. K. H. B. Crown 8vo. 3s. 6d.

Sunday Afternoons at the Parish Church of a Scottish University
City. By A. K. H. B. Crown 8vo. 3s. 6d.

Lessons of Middle Age; with some Account of various Cities and
Men. By A. K. H. B. Crown 8vo. 3s. 6d.

Counsel and Comfort spoken from a City Pulpit. By A. K. H. B.
Crown 8vo. price 3s. 6d.

Changed Aspects of Unchanged Truths; Memorials of St. Andrews
Sundays. By A. K. H.B. Crown 8vo. 3s. 6d.

SHORT STUDIES on GREAT SUBJECTS. By James Anthony
Froude, M.A., late Fellow of Exeter Coll. Oxford. Third Edition. 8vo. 12s.

LORD MACAULAY'S MISCELLANEOUS WRITINGS:—
LIBRARY EDITION. 2 vols. 8vo. Portrait, 21s.
PEOPLE'S EDITION. 1 vol. crown 8vo. 4s. 6d.

The REV. SYDNEY SMITH'S MISCELLANEOUS WORKS; including his Contributions to the *Edinburgh Review*. Crown 8vo. 6s.

The Wit and Wisdom of the Rev. Sydney Smith: a Selection of
the most memorable Passages in his Writings and Conversation. 16mo. 3s. 6d.

TRACES of HISTORY in the NAMES of PLACES; with a
Vocabulary of the Roots out of which Names of Places in England and Wales
are formed. By Flavell Edmunds. Crown 8vo. 7s. 6d.

ESSAYS selected from CONTRIBUTIONS to the *Edinburgh Review*.
By Henry Rogers. Second Edition. 3 vols. fcp. 21s.

Reason and Faith, their Claims and Conflicts. By the same Author.
New Edition, accompanied by several other Essays. Crown 8vo. 6s. 6d.

The Eclipse of Faith; or, a Visit to a Religious Sceptic. By the
same Author. Twelfth Edition. Fcp. 5s.

Defence of the Eclipse of Faith, by its Author; a rejoinder to Dr.
Newman's *Reply*. Third Edition. Fcp. 3s. 6d.

Selections from the Correspondence of R. E. H. Greyson. By the
same Author. Third Edition. Crown 8vo. 7s. 6d.

FAMILIES of SPEECH. Four Lectures delivered at the Royal
Institution of Great Britain. By the Rev. F. W. Farrar, M.A. F.R.S.
late Fellow of Trinity College, Cambridge. Post 8vo. with Two Maps, 5s. 6d.

CHIPS from a GERMAN WORKSHOP; being Essays on the Science of Religion, and on Mythology, Traditions, and Customs. By MAX MÜLLER, M.A. Fellow of All Souls College, Oxford. Second Edition, revised, with an Index. 2 vols. 8vo. 24s.

ANALYSIS of the PHENOMENA of the HUMAN MIND. By JAMES MILL. A New Edition, with Notes, Illustrative and Critical, by ALEXANDER BAIN, ANDREW FINDLATER, and GEORGE GROTE. Edited, with additional Notes, by JOHN STUART MILL. 2 vols. 8vo. price 28s.

An **INTRODUCTION to MENTAL PHILOSOPHY**, on the Inductive Method. By J. D. MORELL, M.A. LL.D. 8vo. 12s.

ELEMENTS of PSYCHOLOGY, containing the Analysis of the Intellectual Powers. By the same Author. Post 8vo. 7s. 6d.

The SECRET of HEGEL: being the Hegelian System in Origin, Principle, Form, and Matter. By J. H. STIRLING. 2 vols. 8vo. 28s.

The SENSES and the INTELLECT. By ALEXANDER BAIN, M.D. Professor of Logic in the University of Aberdeen. Third Edition. 8vo. 15s.

The EMOTIONS and the WILL. By the same Author. Second Edition. 8vo. 15s.

On the **STUDY of CHARACTER**, including an Estimate of Phrenology. By the same Author. 8vo. 9s.

MENTAL and MORAL SCIENCE: a Compendium of Psychology and Ethics. By the same Author. Second Edition. Crown 8vo. 10s. 6d.

LOGIC, DEDUCTIVE and INDUCTIVE. By the same Author. In Two Parts, crown 8vo. 10s. 6d. Each Part may be had separately:—
PART I. *Deduction*, 4s. PART II. *Induction*, 6s. 6d.

TIME and SPACE; a Metaphysical Essay. By SHADWORTH H. HODGSON. (This work covers the whole ground of Speculative Philosophy.) 8vo. price 16s.

The Theory of Practice; an Ethical Inquiry. By the same Author. (This work, in conjunction with the foregoing, completes a system of Philosophy.) 2 vols. 8vo. price 24s.

STRONG AND FREE; or, First Steps towards Social Science. By the Author of ' My Life, and What shall I do with it?' 8vo. price 10s. 6d.

The PHILOSOPHY of NECESSITY; or, Natural Law as applicable to Mental, Moral, and Social Science. By CHARLES BRAY. Second Edition. 8vo. 9s.

The Education of the Feelings and Affections. By the same Author. Third Edition. 8vo. 3s. 6d.

On **Force, its Mental and Moral Correlates.** By the same Author. 8vo. 4s.

CHARACTERISTICS of MEN, MANNERS, OPINIONS, TIMES. By ANTHONY, Third Earl of SHAFTESBURY. Published from the Edition of 1713, with Engravings designed by the Author; and edited, with Marginal Analysis, Notes, and Illustrations, by the Rev. W. M. HATCH, M.A. Fellow of New College, Oxford. 3 vols. 8vo. VOL. I. price 14s.

A **TREATISE on HUMAN NATURE**; being an Attempt to Introduce the Experimental Method of Reasoning into Moral Subjects. By DAVID HUME. Edited, with a Preliminary Dissertation and Notes, by T. H. GREEN, Fellow, and T. H. GROSE, late Scholar, of Balliol College, Oxford.
[*In the press.*

ESSAYS MORAL, POLITICAL, and LITERARY. By DAVID HUME. By the same Editors. [*In the press.*

Astronomy, Meteorology, Popular Geography, &c.

OUTLINES of ASTRONOMY. By Sir J. F. W. HERSCHEL, Bart. M.A. Tenth Edition, revised; with 9 Plates and many Woodcuts. 8vo. 18s.

OTHER WORLDS THAN OURS; the Plurality of Worlds Studied under the Light of Recent Scientific Researches. By RICHARD A. PROCTOR, B.A. F.R.A.S. With 13 Illustrations (6 of them coloured). Crown 8vo. 10s. 6d.

SATURN and Its SYSTEM. By the same Author. 8vo. with 14 Plates, 14s.

CELESTIAL OBJECTS for COMMON TELESCOPES. By the Rev. T. W. WEBB, M.A. F.R.A.S. Second Edition, revised, with a large Map of the Moon, and several Woodcuts. 16mo. 7s. 6d.

NAVIGATION and NAUTICAL ASTRONOMY (Practical, Theoretical, Scientific) for the use of Students and Practical Men. By J. MERRIFIELD, F.R.A.S. and H. EVERS. 8vo. 14s.

DOVE'S LAW of STORMS, considered in connexion with the Ordinary Movements of the Atmosphere. Translated by R. H. SCOTT, M.A. T.C.D. 8vo. 10s. 6d.

PHYSICAL GEOGRAPHY for SCHOOLS and GENERAL READERS. By M. F. MAURY, LL.D. Fcp. with 2 Charts, 2s. 6d.

M'CULLOCH'S DICTIONARY, Geographical, Statistical, and Historical, of the various Countries, Places, and Principal Natural Objects in the World. New Edition, with the Statistical Information brought up to the latest returns by F. MARTIN. 4 vols. 8vo. with coloured Maps, £4 4s.

A GENERAL DICTIONARY of GEOGRAPHY, Descriptive, Physical, Statistical, and Historical; forming a complete Gazetteer of the World. By A. KEITH JOHNSTON, LL.D. F.R.G.S. Revised Edition. 8vo. 31s. 6d.

A MANUAL of GEOGRAPHY, Physical, Industrial, and Political. By W. HUGHES, F.R.G.S. With 6 Maps. Fcp. 7s. 6d.

The STATES of the RIVER PLATE: their Industries and Commerce. By WILFRID LATHAM, Buenos Ayres. Second Edition, revised. 8vo. 12s.

MAUNDER'S TREASURY of GEOGRAPHY, Physical, Historical, Descriptive, and Political. Edited by W. HUGHES, F.R.G.S. Revised Edition, with 7 Maps and 16 Plates. Fcp. 6s. cloth, or 9s. 6d. bound in calf.

Natural History and Popular Science.

ELEMENTARY TREATISE on PHYSICS, Experimental and Applied. Translated and edited from GANOT'S *Éléments de Physique* (with the Author's sanction) by E. ATKINSON, Ph.D. F.C.S. New Edition, revised and enlarged; with a Coloured Plate and 620 Woodcuts. Post 8vo. 15s.

The ELEMENTS of PHYSICS or NATURAL PHILOSOPHY. By NEIL ARNOTT, M.D. F.R.S. Physician Extraordinary to the Queen. Sixth Edition, rewritten and completed. Two Parts, 8vo. 21s.

SOUND: a Course of Eight Lectures delivered at the Royal Institution of Great Britain. By JOHN TYNDALL, LL.D. F.R.S. New Edition, crown 8vo. with Portrait of M. Chladni and 169 Woodcuts, price 9s.

HEAT a MODE of MOTION. By Professor JOHN TYNDALL, LL.D. F.R.S. Fourth Edition. Crown 8vo. with Woodcuts, 10s. 6d.

RESEARCHES on DIAMAGNETISM and MAGNE-CRYSTALLIC ACTION; including the Question of Diamagnetic Polarity. By the same Author. With 6 Plates and many Woodcuts. 8vo. price 14s.

NOTES of a COURSE of NINE LECTURES on LIGHT delivered at the Royal Institution of Great Britain in April–June 1869. By the same Author. Crown 8vo. price 1s. sewed, or 1s. 6d. cloth.

LIGHT: Its Influence on Life and Health. By FORBES WINSLOW, M.D. D.C.L. Oxon. (Hon.). Fcp. 8vo. 6s.

A TREATISE on ELECTRICITY, in Theory and Practice. By A. DE LA RIVE, Prof. in the Academy of Geneva. Translated by C. V. WALKER, F.R.S. 3 vols. 8vo. with Woodcuts, £3 13s.

The CORRELATION of PHYSICAL FORCES. By W. R. GROVE, Q.C. V.P.R.S. Fifth Edition, revised, and followed by a Discourse on Continuity. 8vo. 10s. 6d. The Discourse on Continuity, separately, 2s. 6d.

MANUAL of GEOLOGY. By S. HAUGHTON, M.D. F.R.S. Revised Edition, with 66 Woodcuts. Fcp. 7s. 6d.

A GUIDE to GEOLOGY. By J. PHILLIPS, M.A. Professor of Geology in the University of Oxford. Fifth Edition, with Plates. Fcp. 4s.

The STUDENT'S MANUAL of ZOOLOGY and COMPARATIVE PHYSIOLOGY. By J. BURNEY YEO, M.R. Resident Medical Tutor and Lecturer on Animal Physiology in King's College, London. [Nearly ready.

VAN DER HOEVEN'S HANDBOOK of ZOOLOGY. Translated from the Second Dutch Edition by the Rev. W. CLARK, M.D. F.R.S. 2 vols. 8vo. with 24 Plates of Figures, 60s.

Professor OWEN'S LECTURES on the COMPARATIVE ANATOMY and Physiology of the Invertebrate Animals. Second Edition, with 235 Woodcuts. 8vo. 21s.

The COMPARATIVE ANATOMY and PHYSIOLOGY of the VERTE-brate Animals. By RICHARD OWEN, F.R.S. D.C.L. With 1,472 Woodcuts. 3 vols. 8vo. £3 13s. 6d.

The ORIGIN of CIVILISATION and the PRIMITIVE CONDITION of MAN; Mental and Social Condition of Savages. By Sir JOHN LUBBOCK, Bart. M.P. F.R.S. 8vo. with numerous Illustrations. [Nearly ready.

The PRIMITIVE INHABITANTS of SCANDINAVIA: containing a Description of the Implements, Dwellings, Tombs, and Mode of Living of the Savages in the North of Europe during the Stone Age. By SVEN NILSSON. With 16 Plates of Figures and 3 Woodcuts. 8vo. 18s.

BIBLE ANIMALS; being a Description of every Living Creature mentioned in the Scriptures, from the Ape to the Coral. By the Rev. J. G. WOOD, M.A. F.L.S. With about 100 Vignettes on Wood, 8vo. 21s.

HOMES WITHOUT HANDS: a Description of the Habitations of Animals, classed according to their Principle of Construction. By Rev. J. G. WOOD, M.A. F.L.S. With about 140 Vignettes on Wood, 8vo. 21s.

A FAMILIAR HISTORY of BIRDS. By E. STANLEY, D.D. F.R.S. late Lord Bishop of Norwich. Seventh Edition, with Woodcuts. Fcp. 3s. 6d.

The **HARMONIES of NATURE** and **UNITY of CREATION**. By Dr. GEORGE HARTWIG. 8vo. with numerous Illustrations, 18s.

The **SEA and its LIVING WONDERS**. By the same Author. Third (English) Edition. 8vo. with many Illustrations, 21s.

The **TROPICAL WORLD**. By Dr. GEO. HARTWIG. With 8 Coromo-xylographs and 172 Woodcuts. 8vo. 21s.

The **POLAR WORLD**; a Popular Description of Man and Nature in the Arctic and Antarctic Regions of the Globe. By Dr. GEORGE HARTWIG. With 8 Chromoxylographs, 3 Maps, and 85 Woodcuts. 8vo. 21s.

KIRBY and **SPENCE'S INTRODUCTION to ENTOMOLOGY**, or Elements of the Natural History of Insects. 7th Edition. Crown 8vo. 5s.

MAUNDER'S TREASURY of NATURAL HISTORY, or Popular Dictionary of Zoology. Revised and corrected by T. S. COBBOLD, M.D. Fcp. with 900 Woodcuts, &c. cloth, or 8s. 6d. bound in calf.

The **TREASURY of BOTANY**, or Popular Dictionary of the Vegetable Kingdom; including a Glossary of Botanical Terms. Edited by J. LINDLEY, F.R.S. and T. MOORE, F.L.S. assisted by eminent Contributors. With 274 Woodcuts and 20 Steel Plates. Two Parts, fcp. 12s. cloth, or 19s. calf.

The **ELEMENTS of BOTANY for FAMILIES and SCHOOLS**. Tenth Edition, revised by THOMAS MOORE, F.L.S. Fcp. with 154 Woodcuts. 2s. 6d.

The **ROSE AMATEUR'S GUIDE**. By THOMAS RIVERS. Ninth Edition. Fcp. 4s.

The **BRITISH FLORA**; comprising the Phænogamous or Flowering Plants and the Ferns. By Sir W. J. HOOKER, K.H. and G. A. WALKER-ARNOTT, LL.D. 12mo. with 12 Plates, 14s.

LOUDON'S ENCYCLOPÆDIA of PLANTS; comprising the Specific Character, Description, Culture, History, &c. of all the Plants found in Great Britain. With upwards of 12,000 Woodcuts. 8vo. 42s.

MAUNDER'S SCIENTIFIC and LITERARY TREASURY. New Edition, thoroughly revised and in great part re-written, with above 1,000 new Articles, by J. Y. JOHNSON, Corr. M.Z.S. Fcp. 6s. cloth, or 9s. 6d. calf.

A **DICTIONARY of SCIENCE, LITERATURE, and ART**. Fourth Edition, re-edited by W. T. BRANDE (the original Author), and GEORGE W. COX, M.A. assisted by contributors of eminent Scientific and Literary Acquirements. 3 vols. medium 8vo. price 63s. cloth.

Chemistry, Medicine, Surgery, and the Allied Sciences.

A **DICTIONARY of CHEMISTRY** and the Allied Branches of other Sciences. By HENRY WATTS, F.R.S. assisted by eminent Contributors. Complete in 5 vols. medium 8vo. £7 3s.

ELEMENTS of CHEMISTRY, Theoretical and Practical. By W. ALLEN MILLER, M.D. &c. Prof. of Chemistry, King's Coll. London. Fourth Edition. 3 vols. 8vo. £3. PART I. CHEMICAL PHYSICS, 15s. PART II. INORGANIC CHEMISTRY, 21s. PART III. ORGANIC CHEMISTRY, 24s.

A **MANUAL of CHEMISTRY**, Descriptive and Theoretical. By WILLIAM ODLING, M.B. F.R.S. PART I. 8vo. 9s. PART II. just ready.

OUTLINES of CHEMISTRY; or, Brief Notes of Chemical Facts. By WILLIAM ODLING, M.B. F.R.S. Crown 8vo. 7s. 6d.

A Course of Practical Chemistry, for the use of Medical Students. By the same Author. New Edition, with 70 Woodcuts. Crown 8vo. 7s. 6d.

Lectures on Animal Chemistry, delivered at the Royal College of Physicians in 1865. By the same Author. Crown 8vo. 4s. 6d.

LECTURES on the CHEMICAL CHANGES of CARBON. Delivered at the Royal Institution of Great Britain. By WILLIAM ODLING, M.B. F.R.S. Reprinted from the *Chemical News*, with Notes by W. CROOKES, F.R.S. Crown 8vo. price 4s. 6d.

HANDBOOK of CHEMICAL ANALYSIS, adapted to the UNITARY *System* of Notation. By F. T. CONINGTON, M.A. F.C.S. Post 8vo. 7s. 6d. —CONINGTON'S *Tables of Qualitative Analysis,* price 2s. 6d.

A TREATISE on MEDICAL ELECTRICITY, THEORETICAL and PRACTICAL; and its Use in the Treatment of Paralysis, Neuralgia, and other Diseases. By JULIUS ALTHAUS, M.D. &c. Senior Physician to the Infirmary for Epilepsy and Paralysis. Second Edition, revised and partly re-written. Post 8vo. price 15s.

The DIAGNOSIS, PATHOLOGY, and TREATMENT of DISEASES of Women; including the Diagnosis of Pregnancy. By GRAILY HEWITT, M.D. Second Edition, enlarged; with 116 Woodcut Illustrations. 8vo. 24s.

LECTURES on the DISEASES of INFANCY and CHILDHOOD. By CHARLES WEST, M.D. &c. Fifth Edition, revised and enlarged. 8vo. 16s.

A SYSTEM of SURGERY, Theoretical and Practical. In Treatises by Various Authors. Edited by T. HOLMES, M.A. &c. Surgeon and Lecturer on Surgery at St. George's Hospital, and Surgeon-in-Chief to the Metropolitan Police. Second Edition, thoroughly revised, with numerous Illustrations. 5 vols. 8vo. £5 5s.

The SURGICAL TREATMENT of CHILDREN'S DISEASES. By T. HOLMES, M.A. &c. late Surgeon to the Hospital for Sick Children. Second Edition, with 9 Plates and 112 Woodcuts. 8vo. 21s.

LECTURES on the PRINCIPLES and PRACTICE of PHYSIC. By Sir THOMAS WATSON, Bart. M.D. New Edition in the press.

LECTURES on SURGICAL PATHOLOGY. By JAMES PAGET, F.R.S. Third Edition, revised and re-edited by the Author and Professor W. TURNER, M.B. 8vo. with 131 Woodcuts, 21s.

COOPER'S DICTIONARY of PRACTICAL SURGERY and Encyclopædia of Surgical Science. New Edition, brought down to the present time. By S. A. LANE, Surgeon to St. Mary's Hospital, assisted by various Eminent Surgeons. Vol. II. 8vo. completing the work. [*In the press.*

On CHRONIC BRONCHITIS, especially as connected with GOUT, EMPHYSEMA, and DISEASES of the HEART. By E. HEADLAM GREENHOW, M.D. F.R.C.P. &c. 8vo. 7s. 6d.

The CLIMATE of the SOUTH of FRANCE as SUITED to INVALIDS; with Notices of Mediterranean and other Winter Stations. By C. T. WILLIAMS, M.A. M.D. Oxon. Assistant-Physician to the Hospital for Consumption at Brompton. Second Edition, with Frontispiece and Map. Crown 8vo. 6s.

REPORTS on the PROGRESS of PRACTICAL and SCIENTIFIC MEDICINE in Different Parts of the World, from June 1865, to June 1869. Edited by HORACE DOBELL, M.D. assisted by numerous and distinguished Coadjutors. 8vo. 18s.

PULMONARY CONSUMPTION; its Nature, Treatment, and Duration exemplified by an Analysis of One Thousand Cases selected from upwards of Twenty Thousand. By C. J. B. WILLIAMS, M.D. F.R.S. Consulting Physician to the Hospital for Consumption at Brompton; and C. T. WILLIAMS, M.A. M.D. Oxon. (*Nearly ready.*)

CLINICAL LECTURES on DISEASES of the LIVER, JAUNDICE, and ABDOMINAL DROPSY. By CHARLES MURCHISON, M.D. Post 8vo. with 25 Woodcuts, 10s. 6d.

ANATOMY, DESCRIPTIVE and SURGICAL. By HENRY GRAY, F.R.S. With about 400 Woodcuts from Dissections. Fifth Edition, by T. HOLMES, M.A. Cantab. with a new Introduction by the Editor. Royal 8vo. 28s.

CLINICAL NOTES on DISEASES of the LARYNX, investigated and treated with the assistance of the Laryngoscope. By W. MARCET, M.D. F.R.S. Assistant-Physician to the Hospital for Consumption and Diseases of the Chest, Brompton. Crown 8vo. with 5 Lithographs, 6s.

The THEORY of OCULAR DEFECTS and of SPECTACLES. Translated from the German of Dr. M. SCHEFFLER by R. B. CARTER, F.R.C.S. With Prefatory Notes and a Chapter of Practical Instructions. Post 8vo. price 7s. 6d.

OUTLINES of PHYSIOLOGY, Human and Comparative. By JOHN MARSHALL, F.R.C.S. Surgeon to the University College Hospital. 2 vols. crown 8vo. with 122 Woodcuts, 32s.

ESSAYS on PHYSIOLOGICAL SUBJECTS. By GILBERT W. CHILD, M.A. Second Edition, revised, with Woodcuts. Crown 8vo. 7s. 6d.

PHYSIOLOGICAL ANATOMY and PHYSIOLOGY of MAN. By the late R. B. TODD, M.D. F.R.S. and W. BOWMAN, F.R.S. of King's College. With numerous Illustrations. VOL. II. 8vo. 25s.
VOL. I. New Edition by Dr. LIONEL S. BEALE, F.R.S. in course of publication; PART I. with 8 Plates, 7s. 6d.

COPLAND'S DICTIONARY of PRACTICAL MEDICINE, abridged from the larger work and throughout brought down to the present State of Medical Science. 8vo. 36s.

REIMANN'S HANDBOOK of ANILINE and its DERIVATIVES; a Treatise on the Manufacture of Aniline and Aniline Colours. Edited by WILLIAM CROOKES, F.R.S. With 5 Woodcuts. 8vo. 10s. 6d.

A MANUAL of MATERIA MEDICA and THERAPEUTICS, abridged from Dr. PEREIRA'S *Elements* by F. J. FARRE, M.D. assisted by R. BENTLEY, M.R.C.S. and by R. WARINGTON, F.R.S. 8vo. with 90 Woodcuts, 21s.

THOMSON'S CONSPECTUS of the BRITISH PHARMACOPŒIA. 25th Edition, corrected by E. LLOYD BIRKETT, M.D. 18mo. price 6s.

MANUAL of the DOMESTIC PRACTICE of MEDICINE. By W. B. KESTEVEN, F.R.C.S.E. Third Edition, revised, with Additions. Fcp. 5s.

GYMNASTS and GYMNASTICS. By JOHN H. HOWARD, late Professor of Gymnastics, Comm. Coll. Ripponden. Second Edition, revised and enlarged, with 135 Woodcuts. Crown 8vo. 10s. 6d.

The Fine Arts, and *Illustrated Editions.*

IN FAIRYLAND; Pictures from the Elf-World. By RICHARD DOYLE. With a Poem by W. ALLINGHAM. With Sixteen Plates, containing Thirty-six Designs printed in Colours. Folio, 31s. 6d.

LIFE of JOHN GIBSON, R.A. SCULPTOR. Edited by Lady EASTLAKE. 8vo. 10s. 6d.

The LORD'S PRAYER ILLUSTRATED by F. R. PICKERSGILL, R.A. and HENRY ALFORD, D.D. Dean of Canterbury. Imp. 4to. price 21s. cloth.

MATERIALS for a HISTORY of OIL PAINTING. By Sir CHARLES LOCKE EASTLAKE, sometime President of the Royal Academy. 2 vols. 8vo. price 30s.

HALF-HOUR LECTURES on the HISTORY and PRACTICE of the Fine and Ornamental Arts. By WILLIAM B. SCOTT. New Edition, revised by the Author; with 50 Woodcuts. Crown 8vo. 8s. 6d.

ALBERT DURER, HIS LIFE and WORKS; including Autobiographical Papers and Complete Catalogues. By WILLIAM B. SCOTT. With Six Etchings by the Author, and other Illustrations. 8vo. 16s.

SIX LECTURES on HARMONY, delivered at the Royal Institution of Great Britain in the Year 1867. By G. A. MACFARREN. With numerous engraved Musical Examples and Specimens. 8vo. 10s. 6d.

The CHORALE BOOK for ENGLAND: the Hymns translated by Miss C. WINKWORTH; the tunes arranged by Prof. W. S. BENNETT and OTTO GOLDSCHMIDT. Fcp. 4to. 12s. 6d.

The NEW TESTAMENT, Illustrated with Wood Engravings after the Early Masters, chiefly of the Italian School. Crown 4to. 63s. cloth, gilt top; or £5 5s. elegantly bound in morocco.

LYRA GERMANICA; the Christian Year. Translated by CATHERINE WINKWORTH; with 125 Illustrations on Wood drawn by J. LEIGHTON, F.S.A. 4to. 21s.

LYRA GERMANICA; the Christian Life. Translated by CATHERINE WINKWORTH; with about 200 Woodcut Illustrations by J. LEIGHTON, F.S.A. and other Artists. 4to. 21s.

The LIFE of MAN SYMBOLISED by the MONTHS of the YEAR. Text selected by R. PIGOT; Illustrations on Wood from Original Designs by J. LEIGHTON, F.S.A. 4to. 42s.

CATS' and FARLIE'S MORAL EMBLEMS; with Aphorisms, Adages, and Proverbs of all Nations. 121 Illustrations on Wood by J. LEIGHTON, F.S.A. Text selected by R. PIGOT. Imperial 8vo. 31s. 6d.

SHAKSPEARE'S MIDSUMMER NIGHT'S DREAM, illustrated with 24 Silhouettes or Shadow-Pictures by P. KONEWKA, engraved on Wood by A. VOGEL. Folio, 31s. 6d.

SHAKSPEARE'S SENTIMENTS and SIMILES, printed in Black and Gold, and Illuminated in the Missal Style by HENRY NOEL HUMPHREYS. Square post 8vo. 21s.

SACRED and LEGENDARY ART. By Mrs. JAMESON.
Legends of the Saints and Martyrs. Fifth Edition, with 19 Etchings and 187 Woodcuts. 2 vols. square crown 8vo. 31s. 6d.
Legends of the Monastic Orders. Third Edition, with 11 Etchings and 88 Woodcuts. 1 vol. square crown 8vo. 21s.
Legends of the Madonna. Third Edition, with 27 Etchings and 165 Woodcuts. 1 vol. square crown 8vo. 21s.
The History of Our Lord, with that of his Types and Precursors. Completed by Lady EASTLAKE. Revised Edition, with 31 Etchings and 281 Woodcuts. 2 vols. square crown 8vo. 42s.

The Useful Arts, Manufactures, &c.

DRAWING from NATURE. By GEORGE BARNARD, Professor of Drawing at Rugby School. With 18 Lithographic Plates, and 108 Wood Engravings. Imperial 8vo. price 25s.

GWILT'S ENCYCLOPÆDIA of ARCHITECTURE, with above 1,100 Engravings on Wood. Fifth Edition, revised and enlarged by WYATT PAPWORTH. Additionally Illustrated with nearly 400 Wood Engravings by O. Jewitt, and more than 100 other new Woodcuts. 8vo. 52s. 6d.

ITALIAN SCULPTORS; being a History of Sculpture in Northern, Southern, and Eastern Italy. By C. C. PERKINS. With 30 Etchings and 13 Wood Engravings. Imperial 8vo. 42s.

TUSCAN SCULPTORS, their Lives, Works, and Times. With 45 Etchings and 28 Woodcuts from Original Drawings and Photographs. By the same Author. 2 vols. imperial 8vo. 63s.

HINTS on HOUSEHOLD TASTE in FURNITURE, UPHOLSTERY, and other Details. By CHARLES L. EASTLAKE, Architect. Second Edition, with about 90 Illustrations. Square crown 8vo. 18s.

The ENGINEER'S HANDBOOK; explaining the Principles which should guide the Young Engineer in the Construction of Machinery. By C. S. LOWNDES. Post 8vo. 5s.

PRINCIPLES of MECHANISM, designed for the Use of Students in the Universities, and for Engineering Students generally. By R. WILLIS, M.A. F.R.S. &c. Jacksonian Professor in the University of Cambridge. A new and enlarged Edition. 8vo. [*Nearly ready.*

LATHES and TURNING, Simple, Mechanical, and ORNAMENTAL. By W. HENRY NORTHCOTT. With about 240 Illustrations on Steel and Wood. 8vo. 18s.

URE'S DICTIONARY of ARTS, MANUFACTURES, and MINES. Sixth Edition, chiefly rewritten and greatly enlarged by ROBERT HUNT, F.R.S. assisted by numerous Contributors eminent in Science and the Arts, and familiar with Manufactures. With above 2,000 Woodcuts. 3 vols. medium 8vo. price £4 14s. 6d.

HANDBOOK of PRACTICAL TELEGRAPHY, published with the sanction of the Chairman and Directors of the Electric and International Telegraph Company, and adopted by the Department of Telegraphs for India. By R. S. CULLEY. Third Edition. 8vo. 12s. 6d.

ENCYCLOPÆDIA of CIVIL ENGINEERING, Historical, Theoretical, and Practical. By E. Cresy, C.E. With above 3,000 Woodcuts. 8vo. 42s.

TREATISE on MILLS and MILLWORK. By Sir W. Fairbairn, F.R.S. Second Edition, with 18 Plates and 322 Woodcuts. 2 vols. 8vo. 32s.

USEFUL INFORMATION for ENGINEERS. By the same Author. First, Second, and Third Series, with many Plates and Woodcuts. 3 vols. crown 8vo. 10s. 6d. each.

The APPLICATION of CAST and WROUGHT IRON to Building Purposes. By the same Author. Fourth Edition, enlarged; with 6 Plates and 118 Woodcuts. 8vo. price 16s.

IRON SHIP BUILDING, its History and Progress, as comprised in a Series of Experimental Researches. By the same Author. With 4 Plates and 130 Woodcuts. 8vo. 18s.

A TREATISE on the STEAM ENGINE, in its various Applications to Mines, Mills, Steam Navigation, Railways and Agriculture. By J. Bourne, C.E. Eighth Edition; with Portrait, 37 Plates, and 546 Woodcuts. 4to. 42s.

CATECHISM of the STEAM ENGINE, in its various Applications to Mines, Mills, Steam Navigation, Railways, and Agriculture. By the same Author. With 89 Woodcuts. Fcp. 6s.

HANDBOOK of the STEAM ENGINE. By the same Author, forming a Key to the Catechism of the Steam Engine, with 67 Woodcuts. Fcp. 9s.

BOURNE'S RECENT IMPROVEMENTS in the STEAM ENGINE in its various applications to Mines, Mills, Steam Navigation, Railways, and Agriculture. Being a Supplement to the Author's 'Catechism of the Steam Engine.' By John Bourne, C.E. New Edition, including many New Examples; with 124 Woodcuts. Fcp. 8vo. 6s.

A TREATISE on the SCREW PROPELLER, SCREW VESSELS, and Screw Engines, as adapted for purposes of Peace and War; with Notices of other Methods of Propulsion, Tables of the Dimensions and Performance of Screw Steamers, and detailed Specifications of Ships and Engines. By J. Bourne, C.E. New Edition, with 54 Plates and 287 Woodcuts. 4to. 63s.

EXAMPLES of MODERN STEAM, AIR, and GAS ENGINES of the most Approved Types, as employed for Pumping, for Driving Machinery, for Locomotion, and for Agriculture, minutely and practically described. By John Bourne, C.E. In course of publication in 24 Parts, price 2s. 6d. each, forming One volume 4to. with about 50 Plates and 400 Woodcuts.

A HISTORY of the MACHINE-WROUGHT HOSIERY and LACE Manufactures. By William Felkin, F.L.S. F.R.S. Royal 8vo. 21s.

PRACTICAL TREATISE on METALLURGY, adapted from the last German Edition of Professor Kerl's *Metallurgy* by W. Crookes, F.R.S. &c. and E. Röhrig, Ph.D. M.E. In Three Volumes, 8vo. with 625 Woodcuts. Vol. I. price 31s. 6d. Vol. II. price 36s. Vol. III. price 31s. 6d.

MITCHELL'S MANUAL of PRACTICAL ASSAYING. Third Edition, for the most part re-written, with all the recent Discoveries incorporated, by W. Crookes, F.R.S. With 188 Woodcuts. 8vo. 28s.

The ART of PERFUMERY; the History and Theory of Odours, and the Methods of Extracting the Aromas of Plants. By Dr. Piesse, F.C.S. Third Edition, with 53 Woodcuts. Crown 8vo. 10s. 6d.

Chemical, Natural, and Physical Magic, for Juveniles during the Holidays. By the same Author. Third Edition, with 68 Woodcuts. Fcp. 6s.

LOUDON'S ENCYCLOPÆDIA of AGRICULTURE: comprising the Laying-out, Improvement, and Management of Landed Property, and the Cultivation and Economy of the Productions of Agriculture. With 1,100 Woodcuts. 8vo. 21s.

Loudon's Encyclopædia of Gardening: comprising the Theory and Practice of Horticulture, Floriculture, Arboriculture, and Landscape Gardening. With 1,000 Woodcuts. 8vo. 21s.

BAYLDON'S ART of VALUING RENTS and TILLAGES, and Claims of Tenants upon Quitting Farms, both at Michaelmas and Lady-Day. Eighth Edition, revised by J. C. MORTON. 8vo. 10s. 6d.

Religious and Moral Works.

CONSIDERATIONS on the REVISION of the ENGLISH NEW TESTAMENT. By C. J. ELLICOTT, D.D. Lord Bishop of Gloucester and Bristol. Post 8vo. price 5s. 6d.

An EXPOSITION of the 39 ARTICLES, Historical and Doctrinal. By E. HAROLD BROWNE, D.D. Lord Bishop of Ely. Seventh Edit. 8vo. 16s.

BISHOP COTTON'S INSTRUCTIONS in the PRINCIPLES and Practice of Christianity, intended chiefly as an introduction to Confirmation. Sixth Edition, 18mo. 2s. 6d.

The ACTS of the APOSTLES; with a Commentary, and Practical and Devotional Suggestions for Readers and Students of the English Bible. By the Rev. F. C. COOK, M.A. Canon of Exeter, &c. New Edition. 8vo. 12s. 6d.

The LIFE and EPISTLES of ST. PAUL. By the Rev. W. J. CONYBEARE, M.A., and the Very Rev. J. S. HOWSON, D.D. Dean of Chester:—
LIBRARY EDITION, with all the Original Illustrations, Maps, Landscapes on Steel, Woodcuts, &c. 2 vols. 4to. 48s.
INTERMEDIATE EDITION, with a Selection of Maps, Plates, and Woodcuts. 2 vols. square crown 8vo. 31s. 6d.
STUDENT'S EDITION, revised and condensed, with 46 Illustrations and Maps. 1 vol crown 8vo price 9s.

The VOYAGE and SHIPWRECK of ST. PAUL; with Dissertations on the Life and Writings of St. Luke and the Ships and Navigation of the Ancients. By JAMES SMITH, F.R.S. Third Edition. Crown 8vo. 10s. 6d.

A CRITICAL and GRAMMATICAL COMMENTARY on ST. PAUL'S Epistles. By C. J. ELLICOTT, D.D. Lord Bishop of Gloucester & Bristol. 8vo.

Galatians, Fourth Edition, 8s. 6d.

Ephesians, Fourth Edition, 8s. 6d.

Pastoral Epistles, Fourth Edition, 10s. 6d.

Philippians, Colossians, and Philemon, Third Edition, 10s. 6d.

Thessalonians, Third Edition, 7s. 6d.

HISTORICAL LECTURES on the LIFE of OUR LORD JESUS CHRIST: being the Hulsean Lectures for 1859. By C. J. ELLICOTT, D.D. Lord Bishop of Gloucester and Bristol. Fifth Edition, 8vo. price 12s.

EVIDENCE of the TRUTH of the CHRISTIAN RELIGION derived from the Literal Fulfilment of Prophecy. By ALEXANDER KEITH, D.D. 37th Edition, with numerous Plates, in square 8vo. 12s. 6d.; also the 39th Edition, in post 8vo. with 5 Plates, 6s.

History and Destiny of the World and Church, according to Scripture. By the same Author. Square 8vo. with 40 Illustrations, 10s.

An INTRODUCTION to the STUDY of the NEW TESTAMENT, Critical, Exegetical, and Theological. By the Rev. S. DAVIDSON, D.D. LL.D. 2 vols. 8vo. 30s.

Rev. T. H. HORNE'S INTRODUCTION to the CRITICAL STUDY and Knowledge of the Holy Scriptures. Twelfth Edition, as last revised throughout. With 4 Maps and 22 Woodcuts and Facsimiles. 4 vols. 8vo. 42s.

Rev. T. H. Horne's Compendious Introduction to the Study of the Bible, being an Analysis of the larger work by the same Author. Re-edited by the Rev. JOHN AYRE, M.A. With Maps, &c. Post 8vo. 6s.

HISTORY of the KARAITE JEWS. By WILLIAM HARRIS RULE, D.D. Post 8vo. price 7s. 6d.

EWALD'S HISTORY of ISRAEL to the DEATH of MOSES. Translated from the German. Edited, with a Preface and an Appendix, by RUSSELL MARTINEAU, M.A. Second Edition. 2 vols. 8vo. 24s.

FIVE YEARS in a PROTESTANT SISTERHOOD and TEN YEARS in a Catholic Convent; an Autobiography. Post 8vo. 7s. 6d.

The LIFE of MARGARET MARY HALLAHAN, better known in the religious world by the name of Mother Margaret. By her RELIGIOUS CHILDREN. Second Edition. 8vo. with Portrait, 10s.

The SEE of ROME in the MIDDLE AGES. By the Rev. OSWALD J. REICHEL, B.C.L. and M.A. 8vo. [*Nearly ready.*

The EVIDENCE for the PAPACY, as derived from the Holy Scriptures and from Primitive Antiquity; with an Introductory Epistle. By the Hon. COLIN LINDSAY. 8vo. price 12s. 6d.

The TREASURY of BIBLE KNOWLEDGE; being a Dictionary of the Books, Persons, Places, Events, and other matters of which mention is made in Holy Scripture. By Rev. J. AYRE, M.A. With Maps, 16 Plates, and numerous Woodcuts. Fcp. 8vo. price 6s. cloth, or 9s. 6d. neatly bound in calf.

The GREEK TESTAMENT; with Notes, Grammatical and Exegetical. By the Rev. W. WEBSTER, M.A. and the Rev. W. F. WILKINSON, M.A. 2 vols. 8vo. £2 4s.

EVERY-DAY SCRIPTURE DIFFICULTIES explained and illustrated. By J. E. PRESCOTT, M.A. VOL. I. *Matthew* and *Mark*; VOL. II. *Luke* and *John*. 2 vols. 8vo. 9s. each.

The PENTATEUCH and BOOK of JOSHUA CRITICALLY EXAMINED. By the Right Rev. J. W. COLENSO, D.D. Lord Bishop of Natal. People's Edition, in 1 vol. crown 8vo. 6s. or in 5 Parts, 1s. each.

The CHURCH and the WORLD; Three Series of Essays on Questions of the Day. By Various Writers. Edited by the Rev. ORBY SHIPLEY, M.A. Three Volumes, 8vo. price 15s. each.

The FORMATION of CHRISTENDOM. By T. W. ALLIES. PARTS I. and II. 8vo. price 12s. each Part.

ENGLAND and CHRISTENDOM. By Archbishop Manning, D.D. Post 8vo. price 10s. 6d.

CHRISTENDOM'S DIVISIONS, Part I., a Philosophical Sketch of the Divisions of the Christian Family in East and West. By Edmund S. Ffoulkes. Post 8vo. price 7s. 6d.

Christendom's Divisions, Part II. Greeks and Latins, being a History of their Dissensions and Overtures for Peace down to the Reformation. By the same Author. Post 8vo. 15s.

The HIDDEN WISDOM of CHRIST and the KEY of KNOWLEDGE; or, History of the Apocrypha. By Ernest De Bunsen. 2 vols. 8vo. 28s.

The KEYS of ST. PETER; or, the House of Rechab, connected with the History of Symbolism and Idolatry. By the same Author. 8vo. 14s.

The TYPES of GENESIS, briefly considered as Revealing the Development of Human Nature. By Andrew Jukes. Second Edition. Crown 8vo. 7s. 6d.

The Second Death and the Restitution of All Things, with some Preliminary Remarks on the Nature and Inspiration of Holy Scripture. By the same Author. Second Edition. Crown 8vo. 3s. 6d.

A VIEW of the SCRIPTURE REVELATIONS CONCERNING a FUTURE STATE. By Richard Whately, D.D. late Archbishop of Dublin. Ninth Edition. Fcp. 8vo. 5s.

The POWER of the SOUL over the BODY. By George Moore, M.D. M.R.C.P.L. &c. Sixth Edition. Crown 8vo. 8s. 6d.

THOUGHTS for the AGE. By Elizabeth M. Sewell, Author of 'Amy Herbert' &c. Fcp. 8vo. price 5s.

Passing Thoughts on Religion. By the same Author. Fcp. 8vo. 3s.

Self-Examination before Confirmation. By the same Author. 32mo. price 1s. 6d.

Readings for a Month Preparatory to Confirmation, from Writers of the Early and English Church. By the same Author. Fcp. 4s.

Readings for Every Day in Lent, compiled from the Writings of Bishop Jeremy Taylor. By the same Author. Fcp. 5s.

Preparation for the Holy Communion; the Devotions chiefly from the works of Jeremy Taylor. By the same Author. 32mo. 3s.

THOUGHTS for the HOLY WEEK for Young Persons. By the Author of 'Amy Herbert.' New Edition. Fcp. 8vo. 2s.

PRINCIPLES of EDUCATION Drawn from Nature and Revelation, and applied to Female Education in the Upper Classes. By the Author of 'Amy Herbert.' 2 vols. fcp. 12s. 6d.

The WIFE'S MANUAL; or, Prayers, Thoughts, and Songs on Several Occasions of a Matron's Life. By the Rev. W. Calvert, M.A. Crown 8vo. price 10s. 6d.

SINGERS and SONGS of the CHURCH: being Biographical Sketches of the Hymn-Writers in all the principal Collections; with Notes on their Psalms and Hymns. By Josiah Miller, M.A. Second Edition, enlarged. Post 8vo. price 10s. 6d.

LYRA GERMANICA, translated from the German by Miss C. Winkworth. First Series, Hymns for the Sundays and Chief Festivals. Second Series, the Christian Life. Fcp. 3s. 6d. each Series.

'SPIRITUAL SONGS' for the SUNDAYS and HOLIDAYS throughout the Year. By J. S. B. MONSELL, LL.D. Vicar of Egham and Rural Dean. Fourth Edition, Sixth Thousand. Fcp. 4s. 6d.

The BEATITUDES: Abasement before God; Sorrow for Sin; Meekness of Spirit; Desire for Holiness; Gentleness; Purity of Heart; the Peacemakers; Sufferings for Christ. By the same. Third Edition. Fcp. 3s. 6d.

His PRESENCE—not his MEMORY, 1855. By the same Author, in Memory of his Son. Sixth Edition. 16mo. 1s.

LYRA EUCHARISTICA; Hymns and Verses on the Holy Communion, Ancient and Modern: with other Poems. Edited by the Rev. ORBY SHIPLEY, M.A. Second Edition. Fcp. 5s.

Lyra Messianica; Hymns and Verses on the Life of Christ, Ancient and Modern; with other Poems. By the same Editor. Second Edition, altered and enlarged. Fcp. 5s.

Lyra Mystica; Hymns and Verses on Sacred Subjects, Ancient and Modern. By the same Editor. Fcp. 5s.

ENDEAVOURS after the CHRISTIAN LIFE: Discourses. By JAMES MARTINEAU. Fourth and cheaper Edition, carefully revised; the Two Series complete in One Volume. Post 8vo. 7s. 6d.

INVOCATION of SAINTS and ANGELS, for the use of Members of the English Church. Edited by the Rev. ORBY SHIPLEY. 24mo. 3s. 6d.

WHATELY'S INTRODUCTORY LESSONS on the CHRISTIAN Evidences. 18mo. 6d.

WHATELY'S INTRODUCTORY LESSONS on the HISTORY of Religious Worship. New Edition. 18mo. 2s. 6d.

BISHOP JEREMY TAYLOR'S ENTIRE WORKS. With Life by BISHOP HEBER. Revised and corrected by the Rev. C. P. EDEN, 10 vols. price £5 5s.

Travels, Voyages, &c.

NARRATIVE of a SPRING TOUR in PORTUGAL. By A. C. SMITH, M.A. Ch. Ch. Oxon. Rector of Yatesbury. Post 8vo. price 6s. 6d.

ENGLAND to DELHI; a Narrative of Indian Travel. By JOHN MATHESON, Glasgow. With Map and 82 Woodcut Illustrations. 4to. 31s. 6d.

CADORE; or, TITIAN'S COUNTRY. By JOSIAH GILBERT, one of the Authors of 'The Dolomite Mountains.' With Map, Facsimile, and 40 Illustrations. Imperial 8vo. 31s. 6d.

NARRATIVE of the EUPHRATES EXPEDITION carried on by Order of the British Government during the years 1835-1837. By General F. R. CHESNEY, F.R.S. With Maps, Plates, and Woodcuts. 8vo. 14s.

TRAVELS in the CENTRAL CAUCASUS and BASHAN. Including Visits to Ararat and Tabreez and Ascents of Kashek and Elbruz. By D. W. FRESHFIELD. Square crown 8vo. with Maps, &c. 18s.

PICTURES in TYROL and Elsewhere. From a Family Sketch-Book. By the Authoress of 'A Voyage en Zigzag,' &c. Second Edition. Small 4to. with numerous Illustrations, 21s.

HOW WE SPENT the SUMMER; or, a Voyage en Zigzag in Switzerland and Tyrol with some Members of the ALPINE CLUB. From the Sketch-Book of one of the Party. In oblong 4to. with 300 Illustrations, 15s.

BEATEN TRACKS; or, Pen and Pencil Sketches in Italy. By the Authoress of 'A Voyage en Zigzag.' With 42 Plates, containing about 200 Sketches from Drawings made on the Spot. 8vo. 16s.

MAP of the CHAIN of MONT BLANC, from an actual Survey in 1863–1864. By A. ADAMS-REILLY, F.R.G.S. M.A.C. Published under the Authority of the Alpine Club. In Chromolithography on extra stout drawing-paper 28in. x 17in. price 10s. or mounted on canvas in a folding case, 12s. 6d.

PIONEERING in THE PAMPAS; or, the First Four Years of a Settler's Experience in the La Plata Camps. By R. A. SEYMOUR. Second Edition, with Map. Post 8vo. price 6s.

The PARAGUAYAN WAR: with Sketches of the History of Paraguay, and of the Manners and Customs of the People; and Notes on the Military Engineering of the War. By GEORGE THOMPSON, C.E. With 8 Maps and Plans, and a Portrait of Lopez. Post 8vo. 12s. 6d.

HISTORY of DISCOVERY in our AUSTRALASIAN COLONIES, Australia, Tasmania, and New Zealand, from the Earliest Date to the Present Day. By WILLIAM HOWITT. 2 vols. 8vo. with 3 Maps, 20s.

NOTES on BURGUNDY. By CHARLES RICHARD WELD. Edited by his Widow; with Portrait and Memoir. Post 8vo. 8s. 6d.

The CAPITAL of the TYCOON; a Narrative of a Three Years' Residence in Japan. By Sir RUTHERFORD ALCOCK, K.C.B. 2 vols. 8vo. with numerous Illustrations, 42s.

The DOLOMITE MOUNTAINS; Excursions through Tyrol, Carinthia, Carniola, and Friuli, 1861-1863. By J. GILBERT and G. C. CHURCHILL, F.R.G.S. With numerous Illustrations. Square crown 8vo. 21s.

GUIDE to the PYRENEES, for the use of Mountaineers. By CHARLES PACKE. 2nd Edition, with Map and Illustrations. Cr. 8vo. 7s. 6d.

The ALPINE GUIDE. By JOHN BALL, M.R.I.A. late President of the Alpine Club. Thoroughly Revised Editions, in Three Volumes, post 8vo. with Maps and other Illustrations:—

GUIDE to the WESTERN ALPS, including Mont Blanc, Monte Rosa, Zermatt, &c. Price 6s. 6d.

GUIDE to the CENTRAL ALPS, including all the Oberland District. 7s. 6d.

GUIDE to the EASTERN ALPS, price 10s. 6d.

Introduction on Alpine Travelling in General, and on the Geology of the Alps. price 1s. Each of the Three Volumes or Parts of the *Alpine Guide* may be had with this INTRODUCTION prefixed, price 1s. extra.

The HIGH ALPS WITHOUT GUIDES. By the Rev. A. G. GIRDLESTONE, M.A. late Demy in Natural Science, Magdalen College, Oxford. With Frontispiece and 3 Maps. Square crown 8vo. price 7s. 6d.

MEMORIALS of LONDON and LONDON LIFE in the 13th, 14th, and 15th Centuries; being a Series of Extracts, Local, Social, and Political, from the Archives of the City of London. A.D. 1276-1419. Selected, translated, and edited by H. T. RILEY, M.A. Royal 8vo. 21s.

COMMENTARIES on the HISTORY, CONSTITUTION, and CHARTERED FRANCHISES of the CITY of LONDON. By GEORGE NORTON, formerly one of the Common Pleaders of the City of London. Third Edition. 8vo. 14s.

NEW WORKS PUBLISHED BY LONGMANS AND CO.

The **NORTHERN HEIGHTS of LONDON**; or, Historical Associations of Hampstead, Highgate, Muswell Hill, Hornsey, and Islington. By WILLIAM HOWITT. With about 40 Woodcuts. Square crown 8vo. 21s.

VISITS to REMARKABLE PLACES: Old Halls, Battle-Fields, and Scenes Illustrative of Striking Passages in English History and Poetry. By WILLIAM HOWITT. 2 vols. square crown 8vo. with Woodcuts, 25s.

The **RURAL LIFE of ENGLAND**. By the same Author. With Woodcuts by Bewick and Williams. Medium 8vo. 12s. 6d.

ROMA SOTTERRANEA; or, an Account of the Roman Catacombs, especially of the Cemetery of San Callisto. Compiled from the Works of Commendatore G. B. De Rossi by the Rev. J. S. NORTHCOTE, D.D. and the Rev. W. R. BROWNLOW. With numerous Illustrations. 8vo. 31s. 6d.

PILGRIMAGES in the PYRENEES and LANDES. By DENYS SHYNE LAWLOR. Crown 8vo. with Frontispiece and Vignette, price 15s.

The **GERMAN WORKING MAN**; being an Account of the Daily Life, Amusements, and Unions for Culture and Material Progress of the Artisans of North and South Germany and Switzerland. By JAMES SAMUELSON. Crown 8vo. with Frontispiece. 3s. 6d.

Works of Fiction.

LOTHAIR. By the Right Hon. B. DISRAELI, M.P. Fourth Edition. 3 vols. post 8vo. price 31s. 6d.

Nosse omnia hæc, salus est adolescentulis.—TERENTIUS.

NO APPEAL; a Novel. By the Author of 'Cut down like Grass.' 3 vols. post 8vo. price 31s. 6d.

The **MODERN NOVELIST'S LIBRARY**. Each Work, in crown 8vo. complete in a Single Volume:—
  MELVILLE'S GLADIATORS. 2s. boards; 2s. 6d. cloth.
  ———— HOLMBY HOUSE. 2s. boards; 2s. 6d. cloth.
  ———— INTERPRETER. 2s. boards; 2s. 6d. cloth.
  TROLLOPE'S WARDEN. 1s. 6d. boards; 2s. cloth.
  ———— BARCHESTER TOWERS, 2s. boards; 2s. 6d. cloth.
  BRAMLEY-MOORE'S SIX SISTERS OF THE VALLEYS, 2s. boards; 2s. 6d. cloth.

THREE WEDDINGS. By the Author of 'Dorothy,' 'De Cressy,' &c. Fcp. 8vo. price 5s.

STORIES and TALES by ELIZABETH M. SEWELL, Author of 'Amy Herbert,' uniform Edition, each *Story* or *Tale* complete in a single Volume:

  AMY HERBERT, 2s. 6d.   IVORS, 3s. 6d.
  GERTRUDE, 2s. 6d.   KATHARINE ASHTON, 3s. 6d.
  EARL'S DAUGHTER, 2s. 6d.   MARGARET PERCIVAL, 5s.
  EXPERIENCE OF LIFE, 2s. 6d. LANETON PARSONAGE, 4s. 6d.
  CLEVE HALL, 3s. 6d.   URSULA, 4s. 6d.

A Glimpse of the World. By the Author of 'Amy Herbert.' Fcp. 7s. 6d.

The Journal of a Home Life. By the same Author. Post 8vo. 9s. 6d.

After Life; a Sequel to 'The Journal of a Home Life.' Price 10s. 6d.

UNCLE PETER'S FAIRY TALE for the XIX CENTURY, Edited by E. M. SEWELL, Author of 'Amy Herbert,' &c. Fcp. 8vo. 7s. 6d.

VIKRAM and the VAMPIRE; or, Tales of Hindu Devilry. Adapted by RICHARD F. BURTON, F.R.G.S. &c. With 33 Illustrations by Ernest Griset. Crown 8vo. 9s.

THROUGH the NIGHT; a Tale of the Times. To which is added 'Onward, or a Summer Sketch.' By WALTER SWEETMAN, B.A. 2 vols. post 8vo. 21s.

BECKER'S GALLUS; or, Roman Scenes of the Time of Augustus: with Notes and Excursuses. New Edition. Post 8vo. 7s. 6d.

BECKER'S CHARICLES; a Tale Illustrative of Private Life among the Ancient Greeks: with Notes and Excursuses. New Edition. Post 8vo. 7s. 6d.

NOVELS and TALES by G. J. WHYTE MELVILLE:—
The GLADIATORS, 5s.
DIGBY GRAND, 5s.
KATE COVENTRY, 5s.
GENERAL BOUNCE, 5s.
HOLMBY HOUSE, 5s.
GOOD for NOTHING, 6s.
The QUEEN'S MARIES, 6s.
The INTERPRETER, 5s.

TALES of ANCIENT GREECE. By GEORGE W. COX, M.A. late Scholar of Trin. Coll. Oxon. Being a Collective Edition of the Author's Classical Stories and Tales, complete in One Volume. Crown 8vo. 6s. 6d.

A MANUAL of MYTHOLOGY, in the form of Question and Answer. By the same Author. Fcp. 3s.

OUR CHILDREN'S STORY, by one of their Gossips. By the Author of 'Voyage en Zigzag,' 'Picture in Tyrol,' &c. Small 4to. with Sixty Illustrations by the Author, price 10s. 6d.

Poetry and The Drama.

THOMAS MOORE'S POETICAL WORKS, the only Editions containing the Author's last Copyright Additions:—
CABINET EDITION, 10 vols. fcp. 8vo. price 35s.
SHAMROCK EDITION, crown 8vo. price 5s. 6d.
RUBY EDITION, crown 8vo. with Portrait, price 6s.
LIBRARY EDITION, medium 8vo. Portrait and Vignette, 14s.
PEOPLE'S EDITION, square crown 8vo. with Portrait, &c. 10s. 6d.

MOORE'S IRISH MELODIES, Maclise's Edition, with 161 Steel Plates from Original Drawings. Super-royal 8vo. 31s. 6d.

Miniature Edition of Moore's Irish Melodies with Maclise's Designs (as above) reduced in Lithography. Imp. 16mo. 10s. 6d.

MOORE'S LALLA ROOKH. Tenniel's Edition, with 68 Wood Engravings from original Drawings and other Illustrations. Fcp. 4to. 21s.

SOUTHEY'S POETICAL WORKS, with the Author's last Corrections and copyright Additions. Library Edition, in 1 vol. medium 8vo. with Portrait and Vignette, 14s.

LAYS of ANCIENT ROME; with Ivry and the Armada. By the Right Hon. LORD MACAULAY. 16mo. 4s. 6d.

Lord Macaulay's Lays of Ancient Rome. With 90 Illustrations on Wood, from the Antique, from Drawings by G. SCHARF. Fcp. 4to. 21s.

Miniature Edition of Lord Macaulay's Lays of Ancient Rome, with the Illustrations (as above) reduced in Lithography. Imp. 16mo. 10s. 6d.

GOLDSMITH'S POETICAL WORKS, with Wood Engravings from Designs by Members of the ETCHING CLUB. Imperial 16mo. 7s. 6d.

POEMS. By JEAN INGELOW. Fifteenth Edition. Fcp. 8vo. 5s.

POEMS by Jean Ingelow. With nearly 100 Illustrations by Eminent Artists, engraved on Wood by the Brothers DALZIEL. Fcp. 4to. 21s.

NEW WORKS PUBLISHED BY LONGMANS AND CO.

MOPSA the FAIRY. By JEAN INGELOW. Pp. 256, with Eight Illustrations engraved on Wood. Fcp. 8vo. 6s.

A STORY of DOOM, and other Poems. By JEAN INGELOW. Third Edition. Fcp. 5s.

POETICAL WORKS of LETITIA ELIZABETH LANDON (L.E.L.). 2 vols. 16mo. 14s.

GLAPHYRA, and OTHER POEMS By FRANCIS REYNOLDS, Author of 'Alice Rushton, and other Poems.' 16mo. price 5s.

BOWDLER'S FAMILY SHAKSPEARE, cheaper Genuine Editions: Medium 8vo. large type, with 36 Woodcuts, price 14s. Cabinet Edition, with the same ILLUSTRATIONS, 6 vols. fcp. 3s. 6d. each.

HORATII OPERA, Pocket Edition, with carefully corrected Text, Marginal References, and Introduction. Edited by the Rev. J. E. YONGE, M.A. Square 18mo. 4s. 6d.

HORATII OPERA. Library Edition, with Marginal References and English Notes. Edited by the Rev. J. E. YONGE. 8vo. 21s.

The ÆNEID of VIRGIL Translated into English Verse. By JOHN CONINGTON, M.A. New Edition. Crown 8vo. 9s.

ARUNDINES CAMI, sive Musarum Cantabrigiensium Lusus canori. Collegit atque edidit H. DRURY, M.A. Editio Sexta, curavit H. J. HODGSON, M.A. Crown 8vo. 7s. 6d.

HUNTING SONGS and MISCELLANEOUS VERSES. By R. E. EGERTON WARBURTON. Second Edition. Fcp. 8vo. 5s.

The SILVER STORE collected from Medieval Christian and Jewish Mines. By the Rev. SABINE BARING-GOULD, M.A. Crown 8vo. 3s. 6d.

Rural Sports, &c.

ENCYCLOPEDIA of RURAL SPORTS; a complete Account, Historical, Practical, and Descriptive, of Hunting, Shooting, Fishing, Racing, and all other Rural and Athletic Sports and Pastimes. By D. P. BLAINE. With above 600 Woodcuts (20 from Designs by JOHN LEECH). 8vo. 21s.

Col. HAWKER'S INSTRUCTIONS to YOUNG SPORTSMEN in all that relates to Guns and Shooting. Revised by the Author's SON. Square crown 8vo. with Illustrations, 18s.

The DEAD SHOT, or Sportsman's Complete Guide; a Treatise on the Use of the Gun, Dog-breaking, Pigeon-shooting, &c. By MARKSMAN. Revised Edition. Fcp. 8vo. with Plates, 5s.

The FLY-FISHER'S ENTOMOLOGY. By ALFRED RONALDS. With coloured Representations of the Natural and Artificial Insect. Sixth Edition; with 20 coloured Plates. 8vo. 14s.

A BOOK on ANGLING; a complete Treatise on the Art of Angling in every branch. By FRANCIS FRANCIS. Second Edition, with Portrait and 15 other Plates, plain and coloured. Post 8vo. 15s.

The BOOK of the ROACH. By GREVILLE FENNELL, of 'The Field.' Fcp. 8vo. price 2s. 6d.

WILCOCKS'S SEA-FISHERMAN; comprising the Chief Methods of Hook and Line Fishing in the British and other Seas, a Glance at Nets, and Remarks on Boats and Boating. Second Edition, enlarged; with 80 Woodcuts. Post 8vo. 12s. 6d.

HORSES and STABLES. By Colonel F. FITZWYGRAM, XV. the King's Hussars. With Twenty-four Plates of Illustrations, containing very numerous Figures engraved on Wood. 8vo. 15s.

The HORSE'S FOOT, and HOW to KEEP IT SOUND. By W. MILES, Esq. Ninth Edition, with Illustrations. Imperial 8vo. 12s. 6d.

A PLAIN TREATISE on HORSE-SHOEING. By the same Author. Sixth Edition. Post 8vo. with Illustrations. 2s. 6d.

STABLES and STABLE-FITTINGS. By the same. Imp. 8vo. with 13 Plates, 15s.

REMARKS on HORSES' TEETH, addressed to Purchasers. By the same. Post 8vo. 1s. 6d.

ROBBINS'S CAVALRY CATECHISM, or Instructions on Cavalry Exercise and Field Movements, Brigade Movements, Out-post Duty, Cavalry supporting Artillery, Artillery attached to Cavalry. 12mo. 5s.

BLAINE'S VETERINARY ART; a Treatise on the Anatomy, Physiology, and Curative Treatment of the Diseases of the Horse, Neat Cattle and Sheep. Seventh Edition, revised and enlarged by C. STEEL, M.R.C.V.S.L. 8vo. with Plates and Woodcuts, 18s.

The HORSE; with a Treatise on Draught. By WILLIAM YOUATT. New Edition, revised and enlarged. 8vo. with numerous Woodcuts, 12s. 6d.

The Dog. By the same Author. 8vo. with numerous Woodcuts, 6s.

The DOG in HEALTH and DISEASE. By STONEHENGE. With 70 Wood Engravings. Square crown 8vo. 10s. 6d.

The GREYHOUND. By STONEHENGE. Revised Edition, with 24 Portraits of Greyhounds. Square crown 8vo. 10s. 6d.

The OX; his Diseases and their Treatment: with an Essay on Parturition in the Cow. By J. R. DOBSON. Crown 8vo. with Illustrations. 7s. 6d.

Commerce, Navigation, and Mercantile Affairs.

The ELEMENTS of BANKING. By HENRY DUNNING MACLEOD, M.A. Barrister-at-Law. Post 8vo. [Nearly ready.

The THEORY and PRACTICE of BANKING. By the same Author. Second Edition, entirely remodelled. 2 vols. 8vo. 30s.

PRACTICAL GUIDE for BRITISH SHIPMASTERS to UNITED States Ports. By PIERREPONT EDWARDS. Post 8vo. 8s. 6d.

A DICTIONARY, Practical, Theoretical, and Historical, of Commerce and Commercial Navigation. By J. R. M'CULLOCH, Esq. New and thoroughly revised Edition. 8vo. price 63s. cloth, or 70s. half-bd. in russia.

The LAW of NATIONS Considered as Independent Political Communities. By Sir TRAVERS TWISS, D.C.L. 2 vols. 8vo. 30s., or separately, PART I. Peace, 12s. PART II. War, 18s.

Works of *Utility* and *General Information*.

The CABINET LAWYER; a Popular Digest of the Laws of England, Civil, Criminal, and Constitutional. Twenty-fifth Edition, brought down to the close of the Parliamentary Session of 1869. Fcp. 10s. 6d.

PEWTNER'S COMPREHENSIVE SPECIFIER; A Guide to the Practical Specification of every kind of Building-Artificers' Work: With Forms of Building Conditions and Agreements; An Appendix, Explanatory Foot-Notes, and a copious General Index. Edited by WILLIAM YOUNG, Architect. Crown 8vo. [*Nearly ready.*

The LAW RELATING to BENEFIT BUILDING SOCIETIES; with Practical Observations on the Act and all the Cases decided thereon; also a Form of Rules and Forms of Mortgages. By W. TIDD PRATT, Barrister. Second Edition. Fcp. 3s. 6d.

COLLIERIES and COLLIERS: a Handbook of the Law and Leading Cases relating thereto. By J. C. POWLER, of the Inner Temple, Barrister, Stipendiary Magistrate for the District of Merthyr Tydfil and Aberdare. Second Edition. Fcp. 8vo. 7s. 6d.

The MATERNAL MANAGEMENT of CHILDREN in HEALTH and Disease. By THOMAS BULL, M.D. Fcp. 5s.

HINTS to MOTHERS on the MANAGEMENT of their HEALTH during the Period of Pregnancy and in the Lying-in Room. By the late THOMAS BULL, M.D. Fcp. 5s.

NOTES on HOSPITALS. By FLORENCE NIGHTINGALE. Third Edition, enlarged; with 13 Plans. Post 4to. 18s.

The PHILOSOPHY of HEALTH; or, an Exposition of the Physiological and Sanitary Conditions conducive to Human Longevity and Happiness. By SOUTHWOOD SMITH, M.D. Eleventh Edition, revised and enlarged; with 113 Woodcuts. 8vo. 7s. 6d.

WHIST, WHAT TO LEAD. By CAM. Fourth Edition. 32mo. 1s.

CHESS OPENINGS. By F. W. LONGMAN, Balliol College, Oxford. Fcp. 8vo. 2s. 6d.

A PRACTICAL TREATISE on BREWING; with Formulae for Public Brewers, and Instructions for Private Families. By W. BLACK. 8vo. 10s. 6d.

MODERN COOKERY for PRIVATE FAMILIES, reduced to a System of Easy Practice in a Series of carefully-tested Receipts. By ELIZA ACTON. Newly revised and enlarged Edition; with 8 Plates of Figures and 150 Woodcuts. Fcp. 6s.

ON FOOD: its Varieties, Chemical Composition, Nutritive Value, Comparative Digestibility, Physiological Functions and Uses, Preparation, Culinary Treatment, Preservation, Adulteration, &c. By H. LETHEBY, M.B. M.A. Ph.D. &c. Crown 8vo. price 6s.

COULTHART'S DECIMAL INTEREST TABLES at 24 Different Rates not exceeding 5 per Cent. Calculated for the use of Bankers. To which are added Commission Tables at One-Eighth and One-Fourth per Cent. 8vo. price 15s.

MAUNDER'S TREASURY of KNOWLEDGE and LIBRARY of Reference: comprising an English Dictionary and Grammar, Universal Gazetteer, Classical Dictionary, Chronology, Law Dictionary, a Synopsis of the Peerage, useful Tables &c. Revised Edition. Fcp. 8vo. price 6s.

www.ingramcontent.com/pod-product-compliance
Lightning Source LLC
Chambersburg PA
CBHW032156160426
43197CB00008B/940